W9-BNE-877

TO MAKE A DIFFERENCE

Larry Cuban

TO MAKE A DIFFERENCE

Teaching in the Inner City

The Free Press, New York

Collier-Macmillan Ltd., London

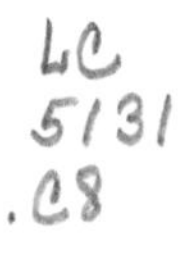

Printed in the United States of America

The Free Press
A DIVISION OF THE MACMILLAN COMPANY
866 Third Avenue, New York, New York 10022

Library of Congress Catalog Number: 74–102197

Printing Number
1 2 3 4 5 6 7 8 9 10

To all the Glenville and Cardozo high school students
and Cardozo Project in Urban Teaching interns
I have worked with—
they have taught me much.

Contents

Part 2 *The Way Things Could Be* 69

Preface

It is not often that a teacher gets a chance to write a book. After all the griping I've done, here was an opportunity to lay out my ideas and perhaps persuade people how I thought education should be. It sounded easy enough and very attractive.

I immersed myself in the literature of education. But within three months, I was paralyzed. Apparently, the decade I had spent in the classroom had been used by many others to read and write about teaching. Overwhelmed by the mountain of words, my confidence slipped in proportion to the time I spent in libraries. But it didn't slip enough for me to chuck it all. Encouraged by those who felt I had something to contribute, I decided to do the best I could with what I knew and felt. And for better or worse, here it is.

I owe many people my thanks. Maxine Daly, Lindley Stiles, and Walter Daniel offered comments on the first three chapters. Dan Levine was most helpful in his critical reading of the first half of the manuscript. My wife, Barbara, endured the late hours of typing illegible drafts and my short temper. Without her patience and grace there would have been no book. Sondra and Janice lent their laughter and vitality in a very important way. Finally, a former principal of mine, Oliver Deex, whom I haven't seen in years but think of often, I thank for stimulating a very green teacher into doing some hard thinking about education. Of course, friends and family are in no way responsible for the flaws that exist in the book. I take the rap for those.

Larry Cuban

October, 1968

Editor's Introduction

The inner-city school, the current phrase for schools populated with blacks, Puerto Ricans, and poor whites, is under the spotlight today. Books, pamphlets, and articles by the hundreds about inner-city schools, teachers, children, parents, and the general environment have been printed during the past several years. Institutes for teachers of the "disadvantaged" or "culturally deprived" have been conducted on college and university campuses throughout the nation. Special teacher-training programs for "difficult" schools have been established by a number of institutions of higher learning. The Teacher Corps has recruited and trained hundreds of young people for service in inner-city schools.

An increasing number of young teachers are dedicated to teaching in schools located in the inner city. Unfortunately, many of them are not prepared for what they find upon entering service in such schools and some become frustrated, angry, bitter, and cynical. These young teachers are not simply seeking to enter the school as a teacher. They are seeking to change the school system for the better. They are seeking what many of us believe is imperative—rapid, and to some educators, radical adaptations and change in schools.

One basic reason why many young teachers are not prepared for teaching is a deficiency in realistic and useful teaching methodology. In this series, *Introduction to Teaching,* teaching methodology includes strategies, techniques, and procedures used by excellent teachers as they provide opportunities and motivation for students to learn. The basic objective, then, of the series is to bridge the gap that exists between highly theoretical and abstract methodology taught in isolated college classrooms in fragmented courses, and the real world and problems, challenges, and satisfactions of the teacher.

Larry Cuban has written a book that draws on a rich background of first-hand experience, especially in the Cardozo Project in Urban Teaching in Washington, D.C. His experience and insight made it possible for him to sort out from research reports and other educational literature relevant and meaningful material to clarify and illustrate his own concepts and analyses of teaching in the inner city. His lucid and candid writing style enabled him to write a book that is readable and makes sense.

A hallmark of *To Make a Difference* is good sense.

The scare literature on inner-city schools is treated in perspective—in fact, it is pretty well debunked. Stereotypes of children from low socioeconomic backgrounds are challenged in a logical and persuasive fashion. One of the almost forgotten or ignored fundamentals of education—provision for individual differences in students—is emphasized.

In this book, an accomplished teacher places responsibility on schools and teachers to see to it that children have opportunities to learn. Rationalizations for "why they can't learn" because of their environment outside the school are found to be unacceptable. The clichés offered as explanations which attribute academic failures of children to "the office," "the system," "the broken home," are recognized as buck passing, not diagnoses and prognoses useful to teachers. Cuban explicitly places on schools and teachers responsibility for teaching and for reasonable academic achievement of students.

A second characteristic of this book is the clear and refreshing language. Little jargon is used. The style is declamatory and the book reads as people talk. The author is scrupulous but not pedantic, candid but not cynical, direct but not preachy. Consequently, the book is vivid, lively, and realistic.

Finally, the roles and responsibilities of the teacher as curriculum builder, implementer, and evaluator are presented. Cuban outlines in specific and concrete terms "how to do it" but he avoids the usual "cookbook" textbook approach. An educational philosophy is developed and illustrated. At the core of that philosophy is the attitude that methods and materials must be matched with individual students *by the teacher.* While good teaching methodology may differ little from slums to suburbs, the point is that most suburban children survive poor teaching more readily than do those in inner-city schools.

To Make a Difference should be of value to teachers in training, teacher educators, and administrators, as well as to veteran teachers. Careful study of Cuban's philosophy and application of it should enhance educators' ability and commitment to fully accept responsibility for curriculum and teaching. Acceptance of that responsibility will not be reflected in "sympathy behavior" or "buck passing behavior" but in effective and meaningful *teaching behavior.* This is the first and indispensable step toward improving teaching and learning in inner-city schools.

B. J. Chandler, Dean
School of Education
Northwestern University

Author's Introduction

The scare literature on inner-city schools[1] multiplies every year. From *Blackboard Jungle* to *White Teacher in a Black School* the outpouring of gloom continues. Incredibly inept teachers, unreachable and unteachable kids, calloused administrators, antiquated facilities add up to a formula for instant commercial success. Some books focus on

1. Inner-city refers to those schools enrolling large numbers of low-income children of both races. For the most part they are racially isolated. I have tried to avoid adjectives that wave a red flag like "lower class," "ghetto," "disadvantaged," "culturally deprived" (or depraved as one teacher informed me), because such

the impossible children; others on the hack teachers and principals who systematically conspire to destroy youngsters. Whatever it is, "slum" schools are portrayed as jungles of violence. Uncontrollable children reign. Learning disappears; such a school is a nasty, alien world. And the public believes every word of it.

Witness the continuing exodus to the suburbs in quest of "better" schools. Or the bitter hostility that greets proposals urging suburban parents to receive Negro youngsters in their schools or to bus their children into predominantly black areas. Even when attempts are made to mend the fractures that exist between city and suburb, white and Negro, the public view prevails.

In 1967, for example, I played a small part in arranging a brief live-in exchange between students of two high schools—one in suburban Maryland and the other in central city Washington. After two months of intensive planning and meetings with youngsters and parents of both races, ten students from the Maryland school agreed to attend the inner-city school and live with ten Negro families less than ten miles away. At the last moment, however, one alarmed

---

labels open sores and close minds. More important, these terms exaggerate the difference between children and ignore their many basic similarities. Certainly, "inner-city" is imprecise and probably euphemistic, but at this point in the growing concern over education for the poor there is no sense in obscuring the issues by using even more loaded, inaccurate words. Furthermore, communication must be kept open since I feel most strongly that the experimentation and ferment occurring in these schools are applicable to *all* youngsters. Using "slum" or a similar label persuades too many readers that the topic is special and irrelevant to other youngsters.

parent withdrew her son from the exchange for fear of his being mugged in school.

The day before the Maryland youngsters left, their classmates farewelled them with "What kind of flowers do you want?" and "Come back alive, if you can." When they returned unscathed and elated and told of their experiences, the similarities and differences they had observed and the fun they had had, their classmates expressed disbelief and unconcern.

The white exchange students fortunately had been able to partially dissolve the imaginary world concocted by the scare literature. Most of their peers and elders, unfortunately, remained blanketed by the fear that initially had pushed them into the suburbs.

We are the prisoners of the stereotypes drawn by the mass media of schools for the poor. (The phrase is really out of Charles Dickens.) How else can one explain the seriousness that meets the proposal of extra compensation ("combat pay" to the cynics) for teachers in these schools? Or the proposal made by one large-city superintendent to bus teachers into the school at 9:00 A.M. (in-service training could take place on the trip, he added) and bus them out at 3:00 P.M., thus preventing incidents from occurring.

Such schemes unwittingly nourish stereotypes and inflate fears by perpetuating the myth that an inner-city school is a jungle and the savages (read *kids*) must first be pacified and then civilized. Furthermore, these schemes only widen the gap between what teaching is really like and what the public, especially prospective teachers, believe it to be like.

Of course, newspapers, films, magazines, and novels don't fantasize completely. Incidents do occur; there are inept teachers and stupid administrators; troubled and hostile youngsters do disrupt classes; facilities and materials are inadequate. The teacher's job is hard and fatiguing. There is a brush stroke of truth in any stereotype but a brush stroke is not the whole picture. There is so much more about inner-city schools than the bizarre and the exotic that make the headlines. There is the dull, monotonous routine that goes unreported. There are the subtle cruelties that the teacher and students inflict upon one another. There is the callousness that develops. And there is the effervescent vitality of diverse young people. These don't make headlines or books or movies.

This book will try to present a more balanced, albeit critical view of inner-city education with a great deal of attention focused upon the teacher, teaching, and the children. Rather than force readers to play detective in trying to discover my point of view, let me state clearly where I stand. My assumptions concern the student, teacher, school, methods, and curriculum materials.

STUDENT

—Though most students seldom work up to their capacity, low-income youngsters have been most seriously underestimated by the administration and faculty in terms of what they can learn and achieve. No evidence exists that poor children, black or white, have any different intellectual potential from that of middle- and upper-income children; they can learn to read, write, compute, reason, and create as well as other children, if taught effectively.

—Low-income youngsters have the same general needs and

values as youngsters with more advantages. While there may be some differences in behavior, the similarities outweigh them and must not be ignored.

—Students learn many things from one another; this reservoir of knowledge and skills should be tapped in as many ways as possible, whether it be by integration, heterogenous grouping, organizational schemes, or teaching methods.

—Many low-income children lack the essential writing, reading, computing, and reasoning skills necessary for effective participation in our society. The school—not the student, his family, their income, or their neighborhood—bears the major responsibility for this inadequacy.

TEACHER

—The teacher is the catalyst in the process of learning; the child, the student body, the family, and the curriculum are all contributing or limiting learning factors but it is the teacher who can make things happen in a classroom.

—Teachers, regardless of race, who combine intelligence, flexibility, creativity, and concern with a broad knowledge of their students, are involved with them, and are free from arbitrary restraints imposed by the school system, can make a difference with low-income youngsters.

—The number of effective teachers, and a core of such teachers exists in most inner-city schools, are sadly outnumbered by ineffective, unconcerned, and ill-prepared persons merely occupying space in classrooms.

—The conventional role of the teacher—i.e., subject specialist teaching five classes a day, or a full day at the elementary level, with extra-curricular activity in addition to all the clerical trivia that burden teaching in an inner-city school —is both anachronistic and self-defeating.

METHODOLOGY

—The teacher-dominated, text-bound, student-recitation type of classroom has not yet met the needs of low-income youngsters or, for that matter, of most children. It has failed to stimulate or educate. Such instruction ultimately alienates students and convinces them that what happens in school is divorced from reality.

An approach that maximizes interaction between teacher and student, between student and student, that draws ideas from students rather than pouring facts into them, will engage children and motivate them to learn.

—Instruction that builds upon the strengths of inner-city youngsters rather than one that concentrates on their weaknesses will result in improved performance.

CURRICULUM MATERIALS

—Most instructional materials in use—textbooks, library books, films, filmstrips, workbooks—are narrowly conceived and pay little attention to the experiences and concerns of low-income youngsters. Such curriculum materials, instead of supporting the teacher, provide another arena of conflict between teacher and class.

—The professional who can best decide what is most effective with his students is the classroom teacher; he should, whenever possible, develop lessons and units (print and nonprint) for his class and thereby make the curriculum responsive to youngsters.

SCHOOL

—The school system functions as a monopoly and, being protected from competition, often lacks the necessary impetus to reform itself.

—There are too many artificial barriers erected by the school system that keep students at arm's length from teachers and reduce learning to dealing with trifles.

—Many of the ills ascribed to students, classroom teachers, and principals can be traced like a red thread to the inherent defects of school systems designed to perform functions that are no longer relevant to the times.

Readers should critically examine these assumptions and question the finality of these statements. Clearly, I'm not dealing in facts but with a distillation of my experiences and of others' combined with some strong preferences and hunches. Unassailable facts are hard to come by in education. In view of the size of the educational enterprise in this nation and the enormous investment of time and money involved, we know precious few answers to fundamental questions: For example: What is intelligence? How do students learn? What really happens in the classroom? What is an effective teacher? We just don't know these answers.

While I am trained as an historian, I had to endure the minimum number of education courses because I wanted to teach. Emerging as a certified teacher, the answers to these questions, and many more, had neatly been filed away to be retrieved once I began teaching. It has taken me over twelve years to unlearn much of the nonsense that was stuffed into me and to realize that what we do know about the act of teaching and learning compared to what we don't know can be placed on the head of a pin.

While research has revealed some promising directions to pursue, tested prescriptions for action have yet to materialize. For years it was the convention among teachers and administrators that the I.Q. test was a fixed measure of native intelligence and a reliable predictor of academic success. Serious reservations about such tests, growing out of research with low-income children, have undermined and buried these "facts." (Unfortunately, the corpse still walks among many schoolmen who still believe that I.Q. is sacrosanct.) I.Q., we have learned, simply tells us where we can begin, not how far we can go, with a particular youngster.

If the big questions remain open, there are some answers, nonetheless, to lesser but just as important questions. For example, what forms of training for prospective teachers are most effective in preparing people to teach in inner-city schools? Or what instructional materials generate interest in youngsters? Or which teaching strategies are most successful with inner-city kids?

In this book, there will be questions raised that will remain unanswered and there will be others raised from which concrete, programatic answers are drawn from my experiences. I leave it to the reader to judge whether the questions and answers are relevant to the issues at hand.

Larry Cuban

TO MAKE A DIFFERENCE

Part 1

The Way Things Are

Even if one visited classrooms extensively and interviewed teachers and principals exhaustively, deciding what the inner-city school is really like remains troublesome at best. Part of the difficulty arises from the sociological formulas that infest the literature of education. With poor kids being discovered by the public less than a decade ago, "culturally deprived" children have emerged less as human beings and more as flat people devoid of life, much like the two-dimensional Egyptian figures on pyramid walls.

After teaching twelve years in a number of "slum" schools and plowing through numerous articles on the "deprived," I just don't recognize the boys and girls I teach as the ones I read about. Ralph Ellison had a similar problem with descriptions of Harlem:

> I don't deny that these sociological formulas are drawn from life, but I do deny that they define the complexity of Harlem. They only abstract it and reduce it to proportions which the sociologists can manage. I simply don't recognize the people of Harlem whom I know. Which is by no means to deny the ruggedness of life there, nor the hardship, the poverty, the sordidness, the filth. But there is something else in Harlem, something subjective, willful and complexly and compellingly human. It is "that something else" that challenges the sociologists who ignore it and the society which could deny its existence.[1]

"That something else" is missing. Simply put, poor children are "compellingly human"; they are not cardboard figures cut out of statistics.

Categorizing administrators, teachers, and schools also is

1. Ralph Ellison, "A Very Stern Discipline," *Harpers,* March, 1967, p. 76.

troublesome. Principals and teachers range from effective to incompetent. There are some schools that create and support learning;[2] there are others that are either maximum security penitentiaries or chaotic child-care factories. Judging how many of one or the other exist and the many in between is risky yet what may be said, but with no real precision, is that a core of imaginative, effective principals and teachers staff many inner-city schools but that these people and schools are all too few and not anywhere evenly distributed. They are oases of competence in a vast desert of ineptitude.

Part I, then, will describe the children, teachers, and the school system as they function in most low-income areas.

2. Effective inner-city schools remain untapped insofar as research is concerned. Integrationists often play the three monkeys; they hear, see, and say nothing about possible achievement gains in low-income schools since they are convinced that little improvement is possible when schools are black and poor. They may be right, but the disturbing fact of varied achievement among schools in a low-income area remains.

Chapter I

The Children

I used to think I was poor. Then they told me I wasn't poor, I was needy. Then they told me it was self-defeating to think of myself as needy, that I was culturally deprived. Then they told me deprived was a bad image, that I was underprivileged. Then they told me underprivileged was overused, that I was disadvantaged. I still don't have a dime, but I do have a great vocabulary.[1]

1. Jules Feiffer, Hall Syndicate, March, 1967, *Reader's Digest*, p. 145.

From reams of paper, oceans of ink, and stacks of articles written on the "disadvantaged," one stubborn fact emerges unaffected by all those words; no one knows for sure exactly who the "disadvantaged" are. What sociologists and educators do know is how to profile statistical groups of youngsters that share the same socio-economic characteristics. They can describe in decimal point detail the environmental, physical, learning, and emotional deficits of poor children. Consider the following list of statements picked at random from the literature on the "culturally deprived."[2]

> They feel like nothing and nobody, unwanted and unnecessary.
> They cannot cope with humiliation.
> They dislike school, often fail and drop out.
> They go to bed hungry, they get up hungry and they go to school hungry.
> They come from a rural background.
> They are retarded in reading.
> They know they are all failures and they are convinced they always will be.
> They are often uncommitted to the larger society and uncontrolled by its values.
> They have been rejected and discouraged too many times to have any ideas of hope or ambition.
> Most disadvantaged children are members of families with many problems; divorce, desertion, unemployment, chronic illness, mental illness, etc.
> Many are unable to speak in whole sentences. Their use of language is restricted.[3]

2. The term is patronizing since it implies at best a hierarchy of culture, or at worst that certain groups of people have no culture at all.

3. Taken from Allan Ornstein in "Who Are the Disadvan-

Scholarly research on the environmental, emotional, and intellectual characteristics of youngsters out of which these statements were taken, unhappily, tell us nothing. They tell us nothing about the diversity of children and they tell us nothing about the individual youngster.

Read some papers written by sixth-grade Harlem youngsters and measure them against some of these sociological generalizations.

A fable written by a boy:

> Once a boy was standing on a large metal flattening machine. The flattener was coming down slowly. Now this boy was a boy who loved insects and bugs. The boy could have stopped the machine from coming down, but there were two ladie bugs on the button and in order to push the button he would kill the two ladie bugs. The flattener was about a half inch over his head now he made a decision he would have to kill the ladie bugs he quickly pressed the button. The machine stoped he was saved and the ladie bugs were dead.
>
> MORAL: smash or be smashed

Another boy describes himself and his wishes:

> This story is about a boy namely me, who lives in a apartment in and around the slum area. I feel that other people should be interested in what I have to say and just like me, try to do something about it, either by literal or diatribe means. This book is only to be read by men and women boys and girls who feel deeply serious about segregation and feel that this is no joke.

---

taged," *Journal of Secondary Education,* April, 1966, pp. 154–161; Robert Havighurst, "Who Are the Socially Disadvantaged," *Journal of Negro Education,* Summer, 1964, pp. 210–217; William Kvaraceus *et al., Negro Self-Concept* (McGraw-Hill, 1965).

A girl describes her block:

> My block is the most terrible block I've ever seen. There are at least 25 or 30 narcartic people in my block. The cops come around there and tries to act bad but I bet inside of them they is as scared as can be. They even had in the papers that this block is the worst block not in Manhattan but in New York City. In the summer they don't do nothing except shooting, stabing, and fighting. They hang all over the stoops and when you say excuse me to them they hear you but they just don't feel like moving. Some times they make me so mad that I feel like slaping them and stuffing bag of garbage down their throats.[4]

Consider also a fifth-grade classroom in another Harlem school as described by the teacher.

> At 1 P.M. in the classroom my children—sweet, many very bright, little fifth graders this year—are watching rain beat on the windows. Arthur went home at noon—"That wind? Blew and blew! It got right up in my sleeves. I thought it was goin' to blow my coat right off from my back!" The children have spied what he brought back—"That's a Pilgrim pumpkin he's got!" It fascinates them that only the pumpkins, corn, and clams which the Indians had taught them to dig saved the Pilgrims the first winter of 1620. Another fact that especially charms the children is that the Indians, after three days at the Thanksgiving feast, didn't want to go home.
>
> We continue the social studies period. The children read letters they wrote for last night's homework, letters Pilgrim children might have written back to England: "Dear Oceanus" from "Respectfully yours, McConnell." Some chil-

4. Jeremy Larner, "The New York Crisis," in *The Urban School Crisis* (League for Industrial Democracy, 1966), pp. 9–10, 21–24.

dren have burnt their pages around the edges to make them look old. Ralph has whacked little cracks in his with a kitchen knife: "That makes it look really old-fashion. It's a letter you find in a castle or museum or something." Tera Mae has written to "Dear Humility. . . . We lived in holes in the ground with roofs we made from bark. . . . Most of us died the first winter. We were too ill to beary dead people. All but four ladies died." Cornelius reads: "Three months passed, we didn't meet no Indians. Then Squanto walked up to Governor Bradford in the forest and said, 'Welcome, white man, to my land.' "

The children listen alertly. They love getting the facts straight. When we watched a film strip that had Indians peeking from behind trees as dories drew into shore from the Mayflower with women in them, children were calling out, "That's wrong!"

Lucius is a pint-sized audience-breaker, with dimples that nip out from odd places in his face. He comes on very big and strong with his paper but soon is meeting new words he's never seen before, which surprise and please and then astonish him. "The Spe- Speed?—" Lucius mumbles, gets in a new position, tilting the page toward the window for more light. "Sp . . . D . . . Dell—" ("The Speedwell set sail from Delfthaven on the 14th of June" is what has been written on his paper.)

"Who wrote this letter, Lucius?" I ask. His friends call out from different parts of the room: "His brother wrote it"; "His brother, huh! His brother couldn'. I know his brother." At length Lucius admits his text was lifted from the children's encyclopedia—"But I did the handwriting m'self"—and squirms back to his seat next to my desk. (From here he crawls over me all day to get things—from me, Claudia says, jealously. "Don't butt in, Claudia," Lucius tells her.) At his desk he's still reading his Pilgrim letter, still fascinated. ". . . windstruck . . . sh . . . shores of Massa—what's that—Massachus—" he reads to himself.

> Lucius is often absent and brings little explanations: "I was home with the asthma"; "My mother said I was catchin' a headache." Other times he is late. At 10 A.M. on Tuesday we were reading about beavers and otters when he slipped into his seat, began thumbing furiously through the reader. "Would you mind taking your hat off?" I asked him. "I just don' want to waste any more time," he said.
>
> He can also bend his body into many shapes. I was grading report cards. He, pretending to be doing his phonics workbook, really was reading the cards upside down. His eyes and ears registered horror as a U (unsatisfactory) appeared on a card, amazement or joy at an E (excellent) and so on. "What are you doing?" I asked him another time. He had wound himself into a contortion of head, neck, chest. "I'm trying to see if my heart and pulse are consecting." "Oh, are you going to be a scientist when you grow up?" He said, "Probably."[5]

Group descriptions seldom capture the essence of individuals. Current generalizations offer only one narrow dimension of children, as if John Trumbull had painted only the backsides of the signers of the Declaration of Independence. The slice of the "disadvantaged" offered here is deviance. Unintentionally, social scientists have depicted the "disadvantaged," especially black children, in terms of middle-class white youngsters and schools. The result is that discrepancies between established norms of behavior and achievement are seen as abnormalities in poor youngsters.

Stated crudely, the kid is to blame for his use of short sentences, inattention, laziness, low self-esteem, etc., etc. Stated in schoolmen's language, the child's environment is such that

5. Orletta Ryan, "I Get One 'U' My Mother Goin' to Beat Me Till It Rains," *The New York Times Magazine,* February 13, 1966, p. 27.

one can expect him to be inarticulate, self-abnegating, unmotivated, etc., etc.

How tragic it is to link poverty and race to learning disabilities. A clear-cut causal relationship has not been established. To say that if one is poor and black he will probably be unable to learn is nonsense. It denies the achievements of Americans, black and white, who have succeeded academically and materially in spite of poverty, or the thousands of low-income youngsters who have improved their performance when the school environment has changed. Furthermore, it is possible, indeed, probable, that the youngster's "abnormal" behavior and achievement is a response to teachers and an institution ill-suited to his needs. If kids can be labeled "culturally deprived" (C.D. in the literature) then schools can be tagged "institutional failures" (maybe I.F. on diplomas).[6]

Dr. Kenneth Clark, after studying I.Q. and achievement scores of Harlem youngsters from elementary and junior high schools, concluded:

> It is an ironic and tragic inversion of the purpose of education that Negro children in ghetto schools tend to lose ground in I.Q. as they proceed through the schools and to fall further and further behind the standard for their grade level in academic performance. The schools are presently damaging the children they exist to help.[7]

6. Of course, malnutrition, isolation, and inadequate medical care scar children and diminish the possibilities of tapping their abilities. Head Start has revealed enough such scars. Recognizing these debilitating effects of poverty does not, in my mind, cause one to leap to the conclusion that the poor cannot learn because they are poor.

7. Kenneth B. Clark, *Dark Ghetto* (Harper and Row, 1965), p. 124.

John Holt passes on what must be an apocryphal story of the Spanish-speaking Puerto Rican child who entered the New York City schools at the age of seven and within a few years could speak neither English nor Spanish. Recent books have focused upon the destructive influence of the school itself. Titles tell their story: Nat Hentoff's *The Children Are Dying* and Jonathan Kozol's *Death at an Early Age: The Destruction of the Hearts and Minds of Negro Children in the Boston Public Schools.*

One Puerto Rican youth, for example, describes his feelings after contact with what he considers incompetent teachers.

> The worst thing a teacher can do is to make a boy feel like he is losing his pride. . . .
>
> They can kill your pride. They make you feel like dirt and its nothing nice to feel like. . . .
>
> Let's take an example. Let's say, here I am talking about a car, about something wrong with the engine. And I know what's wrong with the engine because I have taken it apart and put it right, right in front of you. I tell you, "This is what is wrong with it. You can fix this part and the car will run." And he'll answer that the car will run without this part, or with it. If I tell him then that he's crazy, then it comes: "Don't tell me I'm crazy. I know what's going to happen. You're the student, I'm a teacher, I'm better than you are."
>
> The teachers can really hurt you if they want to. Like we had a teacher who would write up on the board before we even came in. All the boards would be filled with writing. And he wouldn't explain a thing to us. Every day the same thing—writing but no explanation for the things he wrote. And when the tests came, everybody failed. And then he would criticize us, give us zeros, demerits and all these kinds of crazy things and there was no way of getting to

> him. So we all got in a little group and went down to the principal's office. He didn't believe us. So what we did is, we stopped work. We never worked in that class and the teacher called the principal. We told him. "We won't work because he won't explain the things he writes up on the board and we can't learn unless he explains." Finally they threw out that teacher and they brought in another one. That new one, all he ever did was explain. He never wrote anything on the board. . . .[8]

As so many observers have remarked, in spite of the schools, children survive. In other words, it still is an open question whether poverty, racism, or obsolete schools, or a combination of all three, is the fundamental cause of inadequate learning. The headlong rush by many school systems into compensatory programs to re-tool youngsters in a hasty effort to shape them up for the regular school day (i.e., Head Start, Upward Bound, tutoring, trips, etc.) exposed their assumptions that poor youngsters in some way or another were responsible for not reading well and failing.

Certainly the discrepancies in behavior and achievement between middle-income and low-income children are well documented. But bald generalizations about the poor (stripped of qualification and ambiguity) inevitably filter down to well-intentioned administrators, teachers, and college students and are then grafted upon youngsters. Few educators understand that descriptions are not blueprints for action. Yet because they are impelled to make sense out of the daily reality in these schools, they introduce an excessive number of remedial programs that aim to eliminate academic difficulties by hammering kids over the head with evidence of poor class-

8. Charlotte Leon Mayerson (ed.), *Two Blocks Apart* (Holt, Rinehart and Winston, 1965), pp. 71–72.

room performance, or resort to programs that burst with maternal sweetness in an effort to lift sagging self-concepts.

Not too long ago, I visited a handsomely funded program preparing dropouts for low-level positions with the federal government. Over 150 young men and women between 18 and 21 years of age were crowded into a dozen match-box rooms in a former convent. They took remedial math, English, reading, and a few skill courses like typing for seven hours a day, five days a week, from eight young well-intentioned, but inexperienced, teachers.

One bureaucrat in the project had read somewhere that the "disadvantaged" learn well from programed materials and accordingly had purchased a few thousand dollars worth all geared to the third-grade level. After all, everyone knows that the professional literature underscores the severe reading handicaps of "disadvantaged" dropouts. Naturally, the materials were a flop. Had anyone spent time with the youths they would have clearly seen that they ranged in reading skills from college level to illiteracy. Disinterest (except for payday), apathy, and chaos marked the program from morning to late afternoon.

After spending a day with the program, I was asked by the harried director what I thought. The kindest comment I made, and it took some thinking, because I was angry at the waste of kids' aspirations, was that his organization had spent over $100,000 in three months to manufacture a situation far worse than the most inept public school I knew.

I could cite other programs where love and compassion have suffocated youngsters. The point is that many of these programs that interpret generalizations literally and convert them into formulas are terribly blind to the diversity of low-income children. Such efforts callously bulldoze children's personalities in the name of sociologcal findings. Even if educators never bought Hollywood's picture of inner-city youngsters, they nevertheless have been shamelessly flim-flammed by the generalizations peddled by professional educators and academicians.

Another unfortunate by-product of sociological findings has been the confusing of race and class. The litany of Negro, Negro, Negro (or Puerto Rican, Puerto Rican, etc., etc.) hammers home the very simple but very false equation: All Negroes + All Puerto Ricans + Mexican-Americans + (add the minority of your choice) = Culturally Deprived. How tragic and how stupid! After decades of work to break down primitive stereotypes and confusion between class and skin color (by social scientists, ironically enough), the cult of cultural deprivation has welded the two anew. Thus, a fresh Harvard M.A.T. graduate teaching at a 100 per cent black school attended by a large number of middle-income children was shocked by the decorum in the school, the absence of violence, and the "whiteness" of the students. Exactly who was culturally deprived?

The most damage to youngsters probably results from the condescension and paternalism that emerge, unconsciously I think, out of the advice and programs built upon generalizations that confuse race and color. Consider the case of a dedicated, activist principal who had served fourteen years at an elementary school in a black and Puerto Rican inner-city neighborhood in a large eastern city. Because of the high turnover among teachers, he decided to send out a newsletter based upon his experiences to all the faculty, but especially to his new teachers—those blond-haired, blue-eyed girls who come for a year or two and then get married (perhaps out of desperation). His purpose was to lessen the shock of teaching in a "slum" school for the first time. To keep his PTA informed, he sent along an extra copy to the president.

> Welcome back from vacation time. I hope that you have recharged your batteries and are ready for the challenges of the coming academic year.
>
> Some of you are younger and more spirited than your elder colleagues. It is to you that this letter is primarily addressed. Your more experienced colleagues can corroborate what follows.
>
> Our school receives many special services such as smaller [classes], more money per child, and teacher specialists. Why do we get these special services?
>
> Our children, for the most part, come from homes that are usually disadvantaged. That means that, compared with middle-class homes, they are poorer financially, academically, socially. Specifically, many of our children are on welfare. We serve over 500 free lunches daily. The school lunch is the best meal they get.
>
> Many of our children have no father at home. There can be no organized family activities. There is lacking a male image. The mother is so busy with her brood that the individual child is lonely. He has no conversation with the mother or other adults. He is accustomed to listen. In fact, living in a noisy atmosphere, he has a high hearing level, i.e. he shuts out most noises and sounds in self-protection. Hence he is not going to hear his middle-class teacher who speaks quietly until he has been trained to do so by his teacher who has this as one of her conscious, specific aims.
>
> The language he hears at home may be Spanish. Or it may be poor speech of a parent who is illiterate or of limited schooling. The Spanish child knows that his parents do not speak English so he is more likely to imitate his teacher's speech. The other child acts upon the assumption that his

parents speak English and hence is less likely, possibly, to imitate the teacher. An intense attention to correct speech by your children is most essential.

Furthermore, there is lack of encouragement at home to achieve. There may be absent adequate male models. Families on welfare for the third generation lack academic drive.

The physical situation at home may be deplorable. Cold flats, no hot water, peeling paint and falling plaster, vermin, overcrowding—these are the characteristics of the homes of some of our children. For such children school is an oasis from squalor. You will find that your attendance is highest on the coldest days, for school is clean and warm.

Coming from a poor environment, socially, culturally, economically, physically, it is no wonder that our children are not ready for school when they enter and that, in the case of some of them, there is a cumulative decline in academic achievement as they move along in a school whose staff is middle class and whose values confuse some of the children. Specifically the proper care of textbooks, the keeping of an accurate, neat, complete notebook, punctuality, proper dress and cleanliness are things which we have to teach children and, unfortunately, some parents. These are characteristics of poverty irrespective of ethnic groups. The people of the Appalachian Mountains, the Ozark hill-billies [sic], the Mexican-American migrant farmworkers, have these attributes as well as poor Negroes and poor Puerto Ricans.

One purpose of this letter is to help you rid yourself of certain misconceptions: not "all slum children are slow-learners." Actually, "underprivileged" kids have just as wide range of abilities as middle class kids (Prof. Harry Passow at Teachers College). Hence, you must not have the idea that your role is chiefly custodial—that if you keep them quiet and in their seats you have earned your salary: you haven't. Mere custodians are taking their checks under false pretenses. You have a license as a teacher. That is your job

> —to teach—to teach with all of these difficulties in mind, to try to compensate for their handicaps. If you are indifferent to their academic achievement or lack of it, they will continue to be indifferent, for their poor environment and minority group status are not their fault. Nor is it yours. But it *is* your responsibility to plan your work with these facts in mind. . . .[9]

The copy sent to the PTA created a furor. Parents screamed for the principal's resignation, claiming that he had insulted them and was a racist. Petitions were circulated; local civil rights groups joined the protest; meetings were held. The upshot was that the principal did not resign or request transfer, as he was urged to do. The community was divided and embittered over the incident; the gap between school and neighborhood had widened ominously. Whatever goodwill had built up over the past fourteen years disappeared with that letter.

The reaction of the principal was initially shock and later, resentment—shock because he didn't realize that what he had said was both inaccurate and patronizing. (Notice how he unintentionally blames the youngster and his family for all the school problems.) When asked by the PTA for a public apology, he indignantly refused. His resentment developed shortly thereafter when he reconsidered his dedicated service to the school and his liberal position on civil rights. He had become the butt of criticism that was usually leveled at bigots. And after all he had done for the Negro!

Where had he erred? First, he misread totally the diversity of socio-economic class that exists in segregated neighbor-

9. Estelle Fuchs, *Pickets at the Gates* (The Free press, 1966), pp. 6–8.

hoods. Second, his middle-class prejudices (the ones he warned new teachers about) slipped into the discussion and colored his views of youngsters and parents. Third, he combined sense and nonsense in his descriptions of children and parents by borrowing generalizations from sociology and psychology and applying them uncritically to the children and the community his school serves.

What did his new teachers learn from the memo? Not much, I would guess. Such descriptions, or warnings to be more exact, burden teachers at best or paralyze them at worst. Did he learn anything? Probably. He discovered that he did not know the range of income and style of living of his students and their parents. Unpleasantly, he realized that his views about youngsters had better be re-examined. Lastly, he learned that he shouldn't send memos to the PTA.

Facile sociological "wisdom" must be gingerly handled and in some cases discarded. Goodwin Watson cautioned wisely:

> There may be relatively more fatherless homes in Harlem than Hackensack, but many Harlem children—probably most children—have both father and mother at home. Average reading scores may be low, but some disadvantaged children read voraciously. Not every pupil of Puerto Rican descent is alienated or truant or a discipline problem. Teachers work, not with averages, but with individuals, and the sociological data may or may not help to understand a particular child's needs.[10]

10. Goodwin Watson, "A Critical Evaluation of the Yearbook, 1964," *Journal of Negro Education,* Vol. XXXIII, Summer, 1964, No. 3, p. 343.

But what about sociological generalizations that depict "disadvantaged" youngsters in positive terms? A number of studies, for example, have concluded that:

- Many . . . youths have more understanding and know-how about some social realities than middle-class youths or many teachers.
- Typical experiences of many socially disadvantaged youths . . . nourish realistic know-how and responsible adaptive behavior in difficult, practical circumstances.
- The "down-and-out" often have a very deep and sincere fellow-feeling expressed in pervasive mutual aid.
- Many of the socially disadvantaged develop early in life a great reliance upon themselves and a sense of autonomy and independence.
- The deprived are articulate.
- The deprived value education highly.[11]

While it's easy to wax romantic about poverty and exaggerate its "benefits," as some of these statements seem to do, nevertheless such statements shift the center of gravity from an obsession with weaknesses to an awareness that strengths exist. To that extent, such studies fill out the picture of inner-city youth more accurately. But beyond that, these statements and others like them are not very helpful for the classroom teacher.

Try comparing both sets of statements, positive and negative, with the earlier descriptions of youngsters and come up with a profile of an individual student. The futility of try-

11. Frank Riessman, *Culturally Deprived Child* (Harper and Row, 1962), pp. 25, 75, passim. Eugene McCreary, "Some Positive Characteristics of Disadvantaged Learners and Their Implications for Education," pp. 47–52 in Staten Webster (ed.), *Knowing the Disadvantaged,* Part I (Chandler, 1966).

ing to boil down the diversity of kids into a mold applicable to poor children is self-evident. The fact of the matter is that until social scientists and educators can sort out the variables of race, income, age, and sex as sources of school behavior and achievement, it is a waste of time for teachers and administrators who work with these children to seriously consider such generalizations as useful. Better chew carefully than swallow whole.[12]

While it is useful to have teachers and administrators know about poverty and its effects, it is far more important for faculty and principal to feel in their guts that poverty does not cause children to perform at a certain level in school. Knowledge of poverty and deprivation can easily be (and has been) disguised as an alibi for doing nothing. "Oh, my God," a teacher will say, "the conditions these youngsters live

12. The whole problem of generalizations deserves a few words. I have no quarrel with the necessity for making generalizations; after all, such statements form the basis of the social sciences. The danger has been over-zealously acting upon them in a field that must deal with groups but treat members as individuals. Social scientists have been too eager to permit theories and fragmentary research to invade educational policy-making. It is here that I quarrel with the use of generalizations.

Yet, I am inconsistent. While I'm hard on those generalizations that have filtered down into the school and shape schoolmen's approaches and urge a skeptical, gingerly handling of them, I make and will make throughout this book all kinds of generalizations. In most cases, I use anecdotal and research evidence to support what I state. I can be easily accused of having my cake and eating it. Perhaps.

One test of a generalization is reality. The generalizations I reject, I've tested against what I've experienced and found them wanting; others I have accepted. The ones I make in this book should undergo the same test. Making generalizations is part of the process of inquiry; it cannot be avoided. And I do not avoid it.

under are so terrible I can't expect them to do the work." Excessive use of busy work like the really trivial and irrelevant material often used passes as "meeting the child's needs and capacity." One hears too often, "It's all they can do; what else can you expect."

Confronting teachers and principals with the pathology of poverty, in addition, runs the risk of paralyzing prospective teachers with visions of little prostitutes, muggers, and rapists plying their respective trades in their classrooms. Worse yet, citing grim statistics can instill a rigid mind-set toward the poor. Piling on academic course work in urban sociology and the psychology of poverty for pre- and inservice teachers is an ominous trend unless far more intimate contact between Academe and poor children are built into these offerings. You want to find out about low-income youngsters? Establish relationships with individual kids. I know of no shortcuts. A year in an inner-city school for a freshman or sophomore as a teacher's aide with staff supervision would harvest more knowledge for that student than a shelf full of texts, including this one, authored by so-called experts.

All of this is to say that poor children are diverse and no amount of research or generalization can compress that diversity into a paragraph, chart, or control group.

The "disadvantaged," then, are youngsters from low-income families. They come to school with a broad range of intelligence, aspirations, skill development, and behavior. They happen to be victimized, unfortunately, by poverty and racism.[13]

13. I'm not going to play the game of saying that everyone, rich and poor, black and white, is disadvantaged. While true to a

Because there are many types of urban poor in America, ranging from the employed poor who are trapped by low wages to the multi-problem poor who provide all the taped interviews for peripatetic social scientists—simple labels do not help.

Take any street in a ghetto and you will find a broad mix of people sharing the same values as the readers of this book. Stable and unstable marriages are there; two-parent homes and broken families; law-abiding and criminal behavior; advanced education and illiteracy; the hopeful and the hopeless. If variability is evident among the poor, as among other segments of the population, there remains one fundamental difference: The people on the street or in the project are locked out from achieving these common values by their lack of money—not morality, by racism—not resolve.

Monographs and statistics fail to capture this diversity but the evidence is there, nevertheless. Read about the narrow slice of Puerto Rican poor in Oscar Lewis' *La Vida,* the Appalachian whites in Harriet Arnow's *Doll Maker,* Negro working-class poor in James Baldwin's *Go Tell It on the Mountain* to document the broad human response to poverty and the poor's fundamental acceptance of middle-class goals. (A friend pointed out to me that "middle class" is another

degree, this thinking, logically extended, cancels out everyone's disadvantages. If everyone is disadvantaged then no one is really handicapped. Rather than miss the crucial point which such sophist exchanges inevitably do, I'm underscoring that one of the most serious disadvantages in this society is to be poor and black (or Puerto Rican, Mexican-American, Indian, etc.). It is indeed unfortunate that white, middle-class people must endure a dull education and suffer by being ignorant of other people, but such burdens do not undercut the dignity of the person and virtual existence of the family as poverty and racism do.

contrived label; the values and goals ascribed to socio-economic class are really human values and goals irrespective of income and status. Is it human or middle class to strive for the amenities that a society holds out for its citizens? Is it human or middle class to want the best for your children?)

To know that the students in your class are poor isn't really helpful. It doesn't tell you how capable each child is; it doesn't tell you what books to use. All that information will do is tell you that your kids have parents who are economically poor. No more, no less. What you make of it depends a great deal upon who you are as a person and your competence as a teacher. If ever a platitude deserves some life blown back into it, it is that teachers should treat kids as individuals and begin with them where they are.

Chapter II

The Teacher

Consider the day of David Brown (not his real name), a seven-year veteran teacher in a Midwestern inner-city school. A graduate of the city's teacher-training institution, Brown worked his way through college and is proud of it. On a recent questionnaire, he had replied that he enjoyed teaching although he was uneasy about the low caliber of new students, that he was satisfied with the working conditions, and that he liked the children in the school.

Arriving at 8:30, he signed the time sheet, picked up the keys to his homeroom and the notices in his mailbox. In his room he began reading the daily bulletins. (This year, Brown has the room the whole day; last year he shared it with one other teacher and the year before he "floated" from room to room to teach his five classes.)

BULLETIN No. 27

October 13, 1967

THOUGHT FOR THE DAY

Difficulties strengthen the mind as labor does the body (Seneca).
(Whoever Seneca was, Brown thought, he knew about this school.)

1. Do not admit to class without a note from Mrs. Jones:
   Raymond Miller 417
   Forest Pettigrew 203
   Timothy Calloway 409
   (Pettigrew is in my 4th period class, I wonder what trouble he's in now. His whole family is bad news.)
2. TIME CORRECTION: Senior Class will have rehearsal for the Convocation today at the 2nd period.
   (Well, there goes that class. And I stayed up late last night clipping those pictures for the lesson.)
3. CANDY SALE: Please turn in all your candy money NOW.
4. Varsity football at home. Students with tickets will be excused the 7th period.
   (I figured they'd do that; I didn't prepare for that class anyway.)

TEACHERS:

1. All male teachers are expected on duty at football game today. Mr. Smith will be around with the sign-up sheet.
2. Beginning TODAY daily absence sheets will be placed in

each teacher's box and may be picked up at any time after 11:10. Students will make *no* more deliveries.
(*I guess the kids found another way of cutting class.*)

3. NO teacher is to send a student on an errand outside the school *without express permission* from the office.
4. Faculty meeting next Wednesday. Be prompt. Attendance will be taken.
(*Oh, hell, another afternoon shot. If he reads to us like he did last meeting, I'll walk out.*)
5. Some homeroom teachers have failed to complete attendance cards, Request for Information Sheets, and triplicate program cards for each student. Students are ABSOLUTELY not to fill these cards out. Do not use ball point pens to complete forms.
(*That's me. I'll have to take those damn things home this weekend to finish them.*)
6. The following schedule for the submission of records and reports for upcoming report card grades is listed for the information of all teachers:
Grading period closed on November 9, Thursday.
Thursday, November 9—All attendance cards are due in Room 109 at 9:45 A.M.
Monday, November 13—All Form 40s are due in the Business Office at 8:45 A.M.
Thursday, November 16—Report cards will be distributed to pupils at 2:50 P.M.
Friday, November 17—Form 39s and Form 40s are due in the office at 9:00 A.M.
(*Oh, God!*)

Brown finished the bulletin as his homeroom began to fill up with youngsters. His thirty-seven youngsters are with him about twenty minutes and then they move on to their first period class. He is supposed to provide guidance for members of the homeroom, but rarely does he have time to lift his head from the records he must complete for the office. While he took roll (since it is Friday, more than eight students were absent), the tardy bell rang. Two latecomers appeared. To one who had been chronically late, he assigned an after school detention. He doesn't like the idea of a detention hall, but Brown feared that the others in the homeroom might arrive late if he didn't hand out detentions.

He called the homeroom to order, read the announcements, and asked for comments or questions. Since there were none except for the stout girl in the last row who wanted to go to the girl's room (permission granted), Brown asked all students to take out their books and study or do homework until the bell rang. Some did. Others put their heads down and went to sleep. A few copied homework from one another. And the rest ignored what Brown had said and began talking until sharp glances and mumblings from Brown ended the conversations. Brown runs a tight classroom and is proud of it.

During the remaining minutes of the homeroom period, he wrote assignments on the blackboard for his five classes. He has three eleventh- and two twelfth-grade English classes. Though it seems to the layman that he would only have two different preparations for the twenty-five classes he teaches a week—one for the eleventh grades and the other for the twelfth grades—he really has more. Or at least he did at one time. Two of his five classes are college preparatory, two are general academic, and one is in the business curriculum. When he first began teaching, he spent an enormous amount of time preparing detailed lesson plans, reading background materials, and the like. But the caliber of students changed and academic standards seemed to fall and he got married and, well, he doesn't have five preparations now; he has two. He still feels uneasy about all eleventh graders reading *The Scarlet Letter* and his twelfth graders analyzing eighteenth century poetry but he has learned to live with it.

The first three periods of the day went well enough for a Friday. Two P.A. announcements interrupted his first period class. ("Will June Taylor of homeroom 201 please report to the office immediately" and "There is a blue Mustang blocking the principal's car in the parking lot. Unless it is moved, it will be towed away.") But the interruptions didn't halt the class from answering questions on the character of Hester Prynne that Brown had lifted from an English literature workbook.

He did grow irritated, however, in his third period Business English class when four students left for the nurse's office in the middle of a discussion on symbolism in Alexander Pope's poetry. It wasn't exactly a discussion since only five of the thirty students present were answering the questions that Brown had assigned; the others had not done their homework. What irritated Brown was that of the four who had left, three had been active in the discussion. Now he was left with a small three-way conversation in a class of thirty. Again, it seemed to Brown that the quality of youngsters in the school was deteriorating.

At lunchtime (the teachers' union had secured 40 minutes of uninterrupted time), Brown joined the "gripe" table. A number of veteran faculty members would often spend the period complaining about the latest stupidity of the administration or bizarre incident in school or an encounter with a troublesome youth. Consensus was invariably reached that if parents were more interested in their children, then the teacher's job would be much easier. But Brown always felt uneasy when the griping turned to the parents because he had met so few (only twelve parents had visited him out of 150 students at the last PTA meeting) and guessed that it was difficult for these parents to attend because many were on welfare. His parents, however, while poor, never took handouts.

The next class was a disaster. The homework he had assigned two days ago was still undone by a majority of the class. He gave them a sermon about responsibility, the importance of education for "you people," why laziness leads to dropping-out, and so on, and ordered the whole class to open their textbooks and begin doing the homework. Most of the students complied, including the ones who had already done the assignment, but within ten minutes a few students had their heads down on their desks ("resting my eyes," one student told Brown), and clusters of buzzing kids materialized. Brown rose from his desk and walked back and forth in front of the class for the remaining twenty-five minutes, glaring at individuals when they began talking.

Finally the bell rang and Brown went to the faculty lounge. It was his planning period, which he usually used to grade papers or catch up on homeroom records, but today he didn't feel like it. He needed a smoke. In the men's lounge (it was a school built over fifty years ago and the lounges were still segregated) a few of the men teachers were playing bridge, one was snoring on the divan, and a small group was gossiping about the school. He joined the last group. He stayed for two periods since his last class was excused early. In the middle of the last period of the day, a

P.A. announcement called him to the principal's office, generating some humorous remarks among the loungers.

Brown knew the call had to do with his application to a federally sponsored summer institute for teachers of the disadvantaged operated by a local university. It did. The principal showed him the strong recommendation he had written to the Director of the institute. The principal had singled out Brown as a stalwart of his staff, responsible in fulfilling professional obligations (he turned in most of his reports on time), of high moral character, an effective teacher, etc., etc. Even though the principal had seen Brown teach only twice in seven years and then was in his classes for no more than twenty minutes, he knew that Brown controlled his classes and rarely sent youngsters to the principal's office for disciplinary measures. The principal gave Brown a copy of the recommendation and wished him luck. Just then the final bell rang and Brown returned to his room to clear his desk. At 3:30, David Brown turned in his candy money, signed out, and went to the football game.

THE DAY OF "MRS. SMITH"

Turn, now, to an elementary school located in a shabby inner-city residential area of Negroes and Puerto Ricans in a large eastern city. The teacher is "Mrs. Smith," a tall woman in her late forties or early fifties with graying hair and deeply-lined face. She has a grown daughter. It is Mrs. Smith's first year of teaching. She graduated from a local college many years ago and has picked up the twelve hours of education courses needed to meet the minimal standards set by the Board of Education. Her second-grade class of eighteen children was labeled "difficult" by the principal when he assigned her the class in September. The following account of Mrs. Smith's class was recorded by an experienced observer:

> It is 9:30 and Mrs. Smith is telling the children to hold their hands up so that she may inspect them to see if they are clean. This done, she tells the children to sing their morning song. "This is the way we wash our hands," the children start singing and make appropriate motions as they continue through the various verses. . . .
>
> The song is over and the teacher, thinking to drill them on the days of the week, asks them, "What day is today? What day was yesterday? What day will tomorrow be?" As the children call out the names of the various days, she stops to correct them: "Give your answers in sentences!"
>
> Meanwhile several children are noisily running around the room hitting one another. Others sit in a stupor, apparently quite unaware of their surroundings. In the space of the first ten minutes, the teacher has already used physical force in an attempt to control the children. She actually hurts them physically. However, she has not achieved control of the class. . . . She frequently addresses her noisy, restless, class, saying "When I have everyone's attention and your hands are folded, then I will listen to what you're trying to say." Since this never happens, she never really listens to any of the children during the morning, yet many of them do seem to want to say something to her. . . .
>
> She suddenly turns upon a child who was quietly looking at a book, "Why are you playing with your book?"
>
> Some children in another part of the room then begin to write; the teacher calls out, "We're talking. We're not writing now." Meantime a few children do give her the proper names of the days; however, most of the class is not paying any attention.
>
> "Take out your notebooks," she calls. "We are going to write our morning news. . . ."

Now, at 10:05, Mrs. Smith walks around the room to see if the children are indeed copying the work from the board in their notebooks. Frequently, she approaches a child and asks, "Where is your book?" If the child does not answer, she repeats the question until he or she does. In one case, she repeated it a good six times, each time raising her voice more until she was shouting.

Some children are not copying because they do not have pencils so she tries to persuade other children to lend them one. . . .

One boy is returning with his pass and six children have raised their hands to ask for permission to go to the bathroom. They shout, "Teacher, can we leave the room? Can we leave the room?" Whenever anyone wants Mrs. Smith she is addressed as "Teacher." No one has called her by name yet.

She answers, "Nobody may leave." Nonetheless, in a moment she gives the pass to one of the children who is quick to leave. When he returns, the same commotion begins anew and she hands the pass to another. The pass is always in use. . . .

From the front of the class Mrs. Smith cries shrilly, "Listen, are you going to get into your seats or are you going to stay there?" The children return to their seats. . . .

It is 11:00 A.M. and Ann is being put in the corner. "Put your hands on your head." Mrs. Smith then turns to go through some words on the board. These are part of the vocabulary appearing in the *Dick and Jane* Series of readers. The list numbers from fifteen to twenty words. She reads each word aloud and the children repeat it in unison. Their task is to copy the words down into their notebooks at the same time. A few do. Her reprimands are constant: "Will you please do your work." Or again, "Why are you not writing?" To a third, "Do you want to go to Mr. Selby?"

From the corner the teacher next passes by the observer. "You see what I have to put up with. These children's

> parents have given me permission to beat them because they do not know what to do with them in order to get them to listen. You see that child there? There is no one at home to talk to her." While she is saying this Edward, an Hispano youngster (who had been in the corner in the morning), is constantly striking George, a Negro youngster (who had lent his pencil to Lucille).
>
> A child in the front of the room raises his hand to ask to leave the room. To no avail. Edward is now going around hitting other children; however, each time he hits George, Robert arises and hits him, defending George. The teacher explains to the observer, "Edward really thinks he is helping me. That's why he is hitting other children." Another frequent target for Edward's barrage is Allen.
>
> The teacher points out a boy, Frankie, to the observer, and says in a normal speaking voice, "His father killed his mother. The boy stays with an aunt and thirteen children. The home background of most of these children is simply terrible. They are all emotionally disturbed. They are really problems. They don't understand normal psychology. They only know brute force."[1]

These two cases are examples of ineffectiveness (Brown) and incompetence (Smith). Of course, they do not represent the broad spectrum of inner-city teachers; nevertheless, I feel strongly that they speak for the many teachers in the middle and lower bands of that spectrum. The imaginative, innovative, and competent teacher is there also but he is grimly outnumbered and overwhelmed by plodding, conservative, and ineffectual associates. A later chapter will deal with competent teaching but for now I will describe and analyze the

1. From *Realities of the Urban Classroom* by G. Alexander Moore, Jr. Copyright © 1964, 1967 by G. Alexander Moore, Jr. Reprinted by permission of Doubleday & Company, Inc.

reasons why some teachers are ineffective, because most studies suggest that inferior instruction is a major problem in large urban school systems.

The easiest, and perhaps the most irresponsible, path to follow is to castigate teachers solely for their hack efforts, plug for a pet panacea that will better prepare teachers, and end the book. Were it only that simple. If blaming students for their inadequacies was considered both shortsighted and inaccurate, obviously pinning the blame on teachers may satisfy bitter critics but would probably miss the disturbing complexities that make teaching in inner-city schools so demanding.

Yet accountability of sorts must begin somewhere. There are true believers around (and I count myself among them) who hold that the fundamental fact of learning is to bring a capable adult in contact with a number of youngsters. They would argue that it is this contact in the classroom or elsewhere that should, can, and must produce intellectual and attitudinal changes in youngsters. If this is so—and the evidence has been massive in underscoring the central importance of the teacher, be he Mark Hopkins or anyone else—then teachers must take their share of the responsibility for the abysmal record of failure in many inner-city as well as suburban classrooms. Now it can be argued persuasively that the inner-city teacher, up to now, has never been given a clear shot at truly teaching youngsters, given the narrow view of instruction, burdensome administrative restrictions, professional limitations, and little communication with youngsters. While this is probably true, teachers have been "instructing" youngsters for years and calling it teaching—taking credit for "successes" and blaming kids and parents for "failures"—and children have been in classrooms year in and year out absorbing information—and calling it learning. Both said it was education. Now everyone steers clear of any responsibility for the near-criminal results of education for low-income children.

Studies have confirmed the actual erosion of I.Q. and achievement scores as youngsters move through elementary and junior high school. One participant hearing these figures for the first time at a national conference angrily burst out that "kids go to school to become dummies." Selective service rejection rates for major urban areas testify to what twelve years' confinement of low-income kids in educational institutions can produce. Drop-outs (or push-outs) consistently concur in their lack of interest in school subjects and in the inferior quality of teachers.

In assessing the low level of student achievement, teachers most often point to the low academic caliber of the children, inadequate family background, and poverty as the controlling factors producing inferior performance. Were I to use the same logic in assessing low-level teacher performance then I would point to the low academic caliber of teacher-education graduates entering the profession, the inadequate training they received at their alma maters, and the poverty of imagination and lack of support from the school system as the sources of teacher ineffectiveness.

Let me define in a very fragmentary way what I mean by "effective." (Remember such definitions are pretty variable; examine it carefully.) Effectiveness is stimulating student interest, involvement, and expression in what is being taught and learned (the two are not the same) as opposed to nurturing apathy and isolation. Control of a class is seen as coming from students and teacher, more as a function of the teacher's personality, planning, and materials and not as a nasty task to perform. Effectiveness is listening to children carefully and having the flexibility to change methods and materials, not to follow blindly what others think students must know and do. Effectiveness is communicating clearly knowledge, skills, and attitudes through a broad repertoire of approaches and materials, not merely telling youngsters what they are to know and feel and how they are to perform. The result of that clear communication is the improved performance of youngsters.

Will students who have such teachers learn more? I think so but I'm not sure. What I do know is that those teachers who can't make contact—i.e., arouse interest in intellectual tasks—seldom get beyond the constant tug of war for power in a classroom and the keep-them-fearful-and-bored-with-busywork strategy. Engaging youngsters and then moving them on—at their speed—is an essential first step; nothing will happen unless students' interests are aroused.

That changes must be made is clear when the sad results of ineffective teaching—the bored, restless students of Mr. Brown and the disruptive, unknowing children of Mrs. Smith—are considered. Urgency also requires changes since more and more evidence points to the disastrous influence incompetent teachers have upon poor, segregated children. Middle-income white kids can endure and survive. Exactly why are the Browns and Smiths of large city schools ineffective and incompetent?

SOURCES OF INEFFECTIVENESS AND INCOMPETENCE

If there is any one point that most observers agree upon it is that too many inner-city teachers are inflexible.[2] The recent spurt of enthusiasm for innovation has smacked hard against the spastic rigidity of inexperienced and veteran teachers. Stubborn resistance by many teachers toward technology, team teaching, use of non-professionals, and less reliance upon texts, convinces many that teachers are downright obstinate, if not narrow-minded. After pouring in thousands of dollars into media hardware, new instructional materials, and the like—pedestrian teaching plods ever onward. This irritating inflexibility, however, stems less from a teacher's deep convictions than from a number of interrelated sources.

To begin with, the caliber of teachers—measured by academic performance, verbal ability, creativity—entering and remaining in inner-city schools as compared to their counterparts in middle- and upper-income areas is second-rate.[3] For those with middle- and low-income backgrounds, teach-

2. Just one example, and not an extreme one at that. An elementary teacher refused to let a child color a pumpkin green; orange had to be the color, even though she had just read a poem about small pumpkins being green.

3. To protect myself from a few of the brickbats hurled by outraged colleagues, let me state categorically the exceptions. There are sharp minds in these schools. But they are few, indeed. More encouraging are the signs of change in the influx of bright BA graduates, MAT interns, National Teacher Corps people, and returning Peace Corpsmen. But given these exceptions, which only modify by degree and not at all the substance, the generalization holds. If I can be criticized it is for telling non-teachers what is commonly felt by teachers in the privacy of their lounges and boiler rooms.

ing is often considered another branch of the civil service. More than a few express their obvious distaste for their low-income youngsters by telling them, "I got mine; you get yours."

When the caliber of inner-city teachers is viewed in the larger setting of who enters the profession—i.e., the less scholarly, the less inquisitive, the less aggressive—then what ends up in the inner-city classroom is unprepossessing.

Classrooms staffed by individuals whose backgrounds and training leave them ill-prepared in terms of knowledge, skills, and attitudes for the demanding task of teaching turn their classrooms into kingdoms whose privacy is fiercely protected from prying eyes and ears. Conditioned by authoritarian classrooms in their own education and threatened by changes in routine, criticism of standards, or questioning of procedure, many teachers point to the inferior students or simply affirm that what is being done is what should be done.

Consider, too, how pre-service training at colleges in most instances only inhibits imagination and flexibility when professors—themselves lacking in clinical experience—force-feed potential teachers with the "truths" about children, learning, and teaching. Out of this pipeline thousands of teachers march into classrooms armed with the "principles" of teaching, principles that harden into dogma well before the first child asks to go to the washroom. That universities continue to plug students full of information and concepts (much of it still hypothetical) prior to any meaningful on-the-job experience flies full in the face of the realities of teaching and learning—i.e., we don't know very much about what goes on in a classroom, what is effective with whom, and the learning styles of youngsters. Yet the blitz of information and theory continues.

Teachers so equipped and confronted with all manner of students—physically active, vital, apathetic, bright, "slow"—often cling with steadfast devotion to what they are familiar with and to what they have been taught. They have become victims of tunnel vision and rigid mind-sets. Their academic baggage and blinders compel them to tiptoe along the thin line of conformity ever fearful of the consequences of divergence.

Another link in the chain of inflexibility is the intellectual isolation of teachers. So many promising individuals suffer from intellectual deprivation; their learning has stopped with the completion of their degree. Opportunities to discuss, think, read, and write about techniques and theory are virtually nonexistent. Teaching multiple-content areas to thirty youngsters for six hours a day at the elementary level and scheduling, onerous teacher class loads of upwards of 170 students, two or three subject preparations a day, extra assignments, and clerical trivia at the secondary level conspire to separate teachers from one another, locking them into their rooms (or lounges out of desperation) and preventing any meaningful cooperation or exchange from taking place. Attend a faculty meeting or grab a smoke in the teachers' lounge if you want to sample the formal and informal level of intellectual give and take.

The school system, then, is partially responsible for creating conditions that nourish rigidity in teachers by isolating them and retarding their intellectual growth. No other profession systematically prevents communication among its members as do the schools. Moreover—rigidity is reinforced by the elaborate superstructure of rules that freeze behavior, teaching styles, and performance into a narrow range of response. An inequitable grading system, for example, forces teachers to judge students on the most perverse criteria and play God with their futures. Furthermore, teachers receive all sorts of signals from the schools—from the rule requiring teachers to sign in and out to supervisors inspecting the color schemes on bulletin boards—signals that tell teachers clearly what are the prescribed ways to operate and the particular paths to take in order to advance in the system. (Re-read Brown's bulletin for a few of the clues.)

Thus, an accidental convergence of teacher-education truths reinforced by an institutional operation devoted to efficient operation (but seldom achieving it) constrain teachers to walk the white line.

Finally, the visceral fear of losing control of a class continually lowers the ceiling upon the teacher's imagination and willingness to learn. If there is anything that strikes at the very being of a teacher it is the dread of having students running the show. Losing control means noise that can't be turned off by a stare or a command; it means students ignoring a teacher; it means failure. How ironic that a profession committed to serving the individual student judges practitioners most critically on how well they manage groups of children.

The paranoia teachers and principals develop about control and noise (of course this applies to suburban schools as well) only further strengthens the teacher's determination to maintain the status quo. The "good" teacher is the authoritarian veteran whose very glance throws a blanket of silence over a class;[4] the "poor" teacher is the one whose class can be heard down the hall. Did, for example, your judgment of Brown and Smith have anything to do with the volume of noise? Many principals, supervisors, and colleagues rate teacher competency by the answer to the single question: Can he keep them quiet? It is stupid but it is true.

Ask, then, teachers to innovate. Ask them to use role-playing, more debates, students teaching other students, grouping to maximize interaction—and heads will nod in agreement that such techniques are useful. But exhortation inevitably fails, because within the given classroom structure teachers know that the precarious balance of power in their rooms might well shift from the grade book and hard stare to unpredictable student questions, answers, laughter, noise, and the easy give and take of intellectual exchange. The authority of the teacher might be threatened even more; this is to be avoided like the plague. Herbert Kohl, who in *36 Children* sensitively wrote of his experiences in a Harlem elementary school, admitted that his preoccupation with squeezing perscribed content into the available time grew out of his fear of losing control of his sixth-grade class. As he gained confidence in himself and, more important, saw discipline as a function of teaching and learning and not a Mount Everest to be conquered, he and his students began to communicate with one another. In short, the prevailing equation of silence with learning coupled to the fear of losing control of a class shrink the teacher's willingness to experiment, to see students as individuals, to break through the

4. At a seminar I ran on classroom management to which I had invited experienced teachers to share their advice with interns, one veteran advised all new people not to smile for the first month so that the students will know that the teacher means what he says.

concrete walls that prevent teachers from letting students learn.

If flexibility is one reason why many inner-city teachers are ineffective, another is their conventional view of what is supposed to happen in the classroom. A teacher, as the role is perceived, imparts information; he tells kids what they should know. If he is really "good" he clarifies the information well and amusingly. He determines how much students know and grades them accordingly. He polices large numbers of youngsters; he completes school records. If all these functions are performed efficiently, the teacher is labeled effective.

A principal probably put it more clearly. She was comparing the recent crop of new teachers with the ones of her generation. "Give me a teacher," she told me, "who can really teach."

We were on pretty good terms so I asked her what she meant.

"I want a gal who is on her feet in front of the class talking to the children. Someone who has her class in the palm of her hand. The children will be so interested that they wouldn't want her to stop talking. That's teaching."

Such a narrow view of the teacher's role only reinforces the charge that the school is a knowledge factory with kids coming off the assembly line stuffed with information. When some youngsters emerge half-full then something is wrong, obviously, with the product, and not the process.

Of course, the teacher is expected to perform numerous other roles: set a moral example, be active in the community, participate in school planning, confer with students and parents, take part in professional activities, and so on. While these are expected roles, actual behavior is confined largely to disseminating information, a role forged millenniums ago and given renewed vigor with every Teacher of the Year award. In the face of an enormous knowledge explosion, it is nonsense to think that such an approach is adequate today for either inner-city youngsters or their suburban counterparts. What is especially invidious about this medieval conception of teaching is how it locks school people into placing a high premium upon information they have access to, such as textbooks, workbooks, and films, thereby preventing them from analyzing what knowledge is worthwhile and on what grounds.

Both the school system and university helped shape this role. Large classes, non-teaching duties, "administrivia," and other tasks narrow the teaching role. And the teacher-education institutions contribute by stumping for solid content backgrounds (delivered via lectures) for prospective teachers who, upon graduation, move into their own classrooms and pass on their notes to yawning students. Talk about a cycle of poverty! Yet it is the youngsters who suffer the most. Pity the students who must sit through a school day during which college-educated adults talk 75 per cent of the day. Prospective teachers should spend at least a week in a school going through what kids must endure; perhaps the urge to tell all to students would be repressed once the teacher moves into his own classroom.

At the elementary school level, knowledge is of primary importance but the teacher's role is broadened by a conviction that unless teachers emphasize the Puritan Ethic, Ten Commandments, and Emily Post the kids will grow up to be slobs and good-for-nothings. There is an excessive amount of preaching, moralizing, and lying in an attempt to compensate for the believed inadequacies of the home. (Mrs. Smith and hand washing; Mr. Brown on the importance of doing homework.) When achievement, a very narrow base to measure success but one used most widely, is contrasted with the role of teachers, results speak for themselves. Not until administrators and teachers of low-income youngsters see themselves doing more than talking will students remember what they learned from them instead of how difficult or easy it was to stay awake in class or how harsh or lenient their rules were.

TEACHER ATTITUDES

Beneath much of what has been said about the inferior quality of teaching in inner-city schools is the negative racial and socio-economic attitudes of the teacher. A number of studies have confirmed the simple fact that how a teacher views a student has a powerful influence upon the student's performance.

That teacher expectations are colored by their estimate of children—Is he in a low- or high-ability group? Is he black or white? Is he poor or like me?—has been documented numerous times. From St. Louis where, Samuel Sheppard, a St. Louis public school administrator, parceled out locker numbers (in the 100's) to teachers and reaped larger returns in student performance, to New York, where Kenneth Clark's study of Harlem teachers and administrators underscored the staff's low expectations of youngsters' capacities—the critical importance of the teacher's attitude toward the individual child has been emphasized.

In 1964, Robert Rosenthal, in a celebrated and often cited study, tested eighteen classes in a San Francisco elementary school. Picking at *random* 20 per cent of the children and labeling them "academic spurters," the researcher told teachers of these students who the "bright" ones were and cautioned them not to discuss test results with students or parents. A control group was established but obviously the only difference between the two groups was in the minds of the teachers.

At the end of the school year, the classes were re-tested. In 90 per cent of the classes, the randomly designated "bright" youngsters gained between 10 to 20 I.Q. points over the control group. Teacher expectation, the study demonstrated, could be manipulated and result in increased I.Q. scores for children picked at random. (This experiment and others are detailed in Robert Rosenthal and Lenore Jacobson, *Pygmalion in the Classroom* (Holt, Rinehart and Winston, 1968.)

Furthermore, racial and class feelings color the teacher's perception of his students. In one study, David Gottlieb examined white and Negro teachers for their views of white and black students and found that teachers of both races perceived the children as lacking middle-class qualities—e.g. they were not "cultured," "dominant," "forceful," "poised," "witty," "sophisticated." White teachers, however, tended to view students as unstable and nonconforming to desirable classroom behavior; Negro teachers tended to view youngsters as possessing universal traits of children.[5]

Clark and others have revealed the blatant prejudice of white teachers toward poor, black children. While there are most certainly enough instances of crude and subtle anti-Negro feelings, my experience (for whatever it is worth)

5. David Gottlieb, "Teaching and Students: The Views of Negro and White Teachers," *Sociology of Education,* Summer, 1964 in Staten Webster (ed.), *Educating the Disadvantaged Learner* (Chandler, 1966), pp. 437–446.

in schools with mixed faculties is that socio-economic class and not racial feelings mark the attitudes of teachers toward students. Enough faculty lounge conversations have convinced me that, were I to close my eyes, I could not distinguish the skin color of the teacher speaking. Probably the two factors are so inextricably tied together that trying to unravel them is futile. Consider the following interview with a white teacher about her mixed white and Mexican-American class in a California elementary school. Although it occurs in a rural area, the evidence indicates that too many inner-city teachers share Mrs. S's attitudes toward poor black and Puerto Rican youngsters, but they tend to be less candid.

> *Interviewer:* Do you remember the group of boys that you stopped from running out of the room the other day? I am thinking about the group that made a rush for the door at noon of the day I visited your classroom. I have been wondering why it was that you selected Johnny to take the lead of the group?
>
> *Teacher:* Oh, yes, I remember. Well—I try to follow the strict rule in my room that no one is to leave the room until everything has been put away and the class is excused. Usually the kids are pretty good, but that day those [four Mexican-American] boys were in a hurry to get out to the playground. . . . I remember thinking that the Mexican boys were going to make trouble if I didn't catch them. You know, they just can't follow directions. You always have to tell them what you want done. They seem to have a hard time remembering the rules. Anyway, I thought that if I told Johnny [an Anglo- or white American] to take the lead, they would have a good example of how to act.
>
> *Interviewer:* Was there some reason why you chose Johnny specifically?
>
> *Teacher:* Yes. He was right there, of course. Besides that, I think that Johnny needs to learn how to set a good ex-

ample and how to lead others. His father owns one of the big farms in the area and Johnny has to learn how to lead Mexicans. One day he will be helping his father and he will have to know how to handle the Mexicans. I try to help him whenever I can.

Interviewer: Do you mean that the Mexicans need somebody to direct them?

Teacher: Definitely.

Interviewer: Why?

Teacher: Well, they are not very bright. Besides that they are lazy. No ambition at all. You should hear some of the boo-boos that the Mexicans make around here. A couple of weeks ago one of them plowed up a whole field of brussel sprout plants after he was told to cultivate around them. . . . Even in school we have these same things. You can tell one of them to do something and they will go and do just the opposite. Just can't trust them to do anything right. They are just like children. If you stand there and show them what to do, they will usually do OK, but if you just tell them, well, you can expect *something* to happen.

Interviewer: Is this why you chose Johnny, because you wanted an American pupil to *show* the Mexican boys how you wanted them to act?

Teacher: Yes. That and what I already said.

Interviewer: Do you often choose American children to show the Mexicans what you want them to do?

Teacher: Oh, yes. I usually do. They need help, like I said, and it is good for the American children to learn to take these responsibilities.

Interviewer: The other day you said that most of the Mexican families are poor and sleep on the floor or something. Can you tell me something more about the homes of your Mexican pupils?

Teacher: You just wouldn't believe how these people live. They live in the worst run-down shacks and things. Some of the families live eight or ten people to a room.

Sometimes the parents and the younger children will sleep in one bed and the rest of the children will sleep in the other bed or on the floor. With all that going on, it is no wonder that the Mexican children know about life so early. Their parents go right on having children and the other kids see everything that goes on. It's no wonder that so many of the Mexican girls get into trouble. I guess that they think that this is a normal way for people to act. The homes are really dirty. There is filth everywhere. That is why the kids come to school smelly so much of the time. The nurse tries once in a while to get these people to clean themselves up, but they really don't care. It's really a crime. Somebody ought to do something.

Interviewer: Have you visited very many Mexican homes?

Teacher: I never did go into one of those places. I don't think that I could stand it.

Interviewer: How do you know what the homes are like?

Teacher: Oh, everybody knows what they are like. You are always hearing stories about the Mexicans. Mrs. E, the school nurse, told me some of the things. The rest I learned from people around town. . . . Everybody pretty well knew what the Mexicans were like. . . .[6]

The universality of attitude toward poor, ethnic group members in this country reveals itself in the interview; in other words, one could have easily inserted "Negro," "Puerto Rican," "Indian," wherever Mexican-American was mentioned. Such crude expressions of stereotypes are seldom encountered openly. More subtle versions are masked by labels such as "cultural deprivation." (Compare this interview, for example, with the letter the principal sent to the PTA in Chapter 1.) Crude or subtle, Mrs. S's and Mrs. Smith's remarks

6. Theodore W. Parsons, Jr., "Ethnic Cleavage in a California School" (unpublished doctoral dissertation, 1965, Stanford University), pp. 38–42.

to the observer earlier in the chapter betray middle-class attitudes toward poor people, heavily laced with covert and overt racism. The results in terms of classroom and school climate range from abrasive to patronizing. Such attitudes lower the ceiling of student performance.

When many teachers are confronted with youngsters who *appear* different, unmotivated, and unscrubbed, they recall the sharp and shining faces from their own school days; a welter of negative feelings (including fear) emerge that initiate (unless checked) a downward spiral of a self-fulfilling prophecy. For thinking that the children probably won't be able to do the work is a short step away from youngsters receiving the teacher's non-verbal signals and not feeling able to do the work. The result: inferior performance and a teacher self-satisfied with his success at knowing *these* youngsters. Creating the conditions for failure and then blaming the person for failing is common in our society but we can ill-afford this waste of human potential.

Teacher attitudes influence expectations and expectations can lift or lower performance. The equation isn't airtight but it contains an internal logic that accounts partially for the grim results exiting from inner-city schools.

Origins of ineffectual teaching can be traced, then, to a variety of sources. Inflexibility, narrow conceptions of teaching, and negative attitudes can be followed, like threads, back to three sources: the raw material that enters the profession, the quality of pre- and in-service training, and restraints that the school system imposes upon teachers. These explain, I feel, why too many incompetents exist, and suggest the directions to take in order to staff classrooms with the skilled, effective teachers urgently needed by children from low-income homes.

Chapter III

The School System

Teachers are reasonable people. When confronted by an intolerable situation, they quit in droves. Teacher turnover is a scandal. If doctors, lawyers, architects, and other professionals were afflicted with the mortality rate peculiar to teachers, a national disaster would be at hand. Consider that out of every 100 teachers graduated from college, within ten years only seven will still be in the classroom. Attrition in inner-city schools spirals even higher, running in some cases from 30 to 50 per cent every year. In some schools, faculty members with three years experience are labeled veterans. And yet some educators condemn the instability of poor families.

Why the exodus? The answers vary, but most reasons given by teachers fall into three categories. Teachers leave because they:

——consider the children unreachable and unteachable

——feel the school structure is ineffectual to cope with problems.

——sense their personal inadequacies

Exiting teachers, then, blame kids first (do doctors blame patients?), themselves last, and the system for everything else.

The flight of teachers from the classrooms and especially from inner-city to suburbs, valid reasons or not, is a symptom of the deeper malaise affecting large urban school systems. This illness has three sources: money, racial insolation, and bureaucratic inertia.

Count the dollars taxpayers spend for educating their children. Rich youngsters, allowing for regional and rural-urban differences, are allotted one-third to one-half more money for their education than poor children. Being born in Shaker Heights, Ohio, offers a child an education worth more than $10,000; however, a child born on the east side of Cleveland gets a bargain basement schooling worth only about $7,000.

Right down the line, the differences in spending show up in physical facilities, supplies, teachers, administrators, class size, and social services. Laying out $500 per year on a child simply doesn't buy much on the educational market. Perhaps $1500 can. But to find out, the pattern of metropolitan spending has to shift radically. To speak about equality of opportunity is illusory until the number of dollars spent is linked to the different educational needs of children.

Of course, the current spending deficiency is related to the rapidly increasing racial isolation of children. The suburban exodus has shrunk every city's tax base and created school systems that are more and more segregated. Within the next four years, at least a half-dozen large school systems will have a Negro majority attending segregated schools. Consider that in 1966 54 per cent of Cleveland's school population was black, but 91 per cent of all its youngsters were attending either a white or black segregated school. Chicago is more segregated than most Deep South cities. And, of course, there is Washington, with a Negro school population of 96 per cent. Affluent lily white suburbs with the capacity to spend more ring cities that need more to spend. With white schools turning black over the years, teachers follow parents and students to the suburbs. Standards (however they are defined) change. Carelessness, callousness, and cynicism fill the void.

Superintendents and their boards, in many cases, facilitated racial isolation by permitting middle- and upper-income whites and blacks to transfer to "better" schools, by gerrymandering school boundaries, or by doing nothing. The result has been flurries of "integration" (the transition period between all white and all black) followed by resegregation.

To the poverty of funds and increasing apartheid, add school bureaucracies incapable of meeting the demands of changing times and new generations of youngsters. The middle-class school system that "worked" so well to assimilate millions of immigrants is a dinosaur today unable to perceive that the world has changed.[1]

THE RIGID SYSTEM

This incapacity to change, according to many critics, is the genetic defect in urban school systems servicing large numbers of the ethnic poor. It explains to a large extent why school people had to be pressured into facing up to racial isolation and why school systems have been forced to scream and scratch for more money. Large urban school systems often reacted, seldom initiated. Without external pressure, the schools would have carried on business as usual and the reason is obvious: the public school system is a monopoly.

As a monopoly the public schools do as they wish. Without the cutting edge of competition the schools need not alter existing programs or services. For the poor, this means that no choices are available. Middle- and upper-income parents, white and Negro, can dig deep into their pocketbooks and send their children to private or parochial schools. The poor cannot. They must send their children to the nearest segregated school and accept what they get since no yardstick exists to measure the quality of their children's education. Only when parents realize that their children cannot read or write well or that diplomas are not worth the paper they're written on, do they complain. By then it is too late. Anyway, to whom should they complain? Teacher? Principal? Superintendent? President of the Board of Education? Which

1. It really didn't work that well. A growing economy soaked up the 60 per cent and over dropouts into unskilled jobs fifty years ago; not so today.

one will listen and who will act? The schools are accountable to no one, least of all to the students. Whether the dropout rate is 5 per cent or 95 per cent, federal and state aid will continue to pour in. A monopolistic, highly bureaucratized school system, unburdened by competition, is less concerned with complaints of irate parents who carry little political clout and more sensitive to avoiding waves within the system. Fortunately, parents have begun to make waves.

Inevitably such a system crushes initiative, experimentation, and intellectual ferment. In such an operation, results are unimportant; what is important is conformity. Students, teachers, and principals must follow the rules of the game. Whether anyone learns or anyone teaches is subordinate to keeping the machine moving. As Christopher Jencks put it:

> Every member of the organization is concerned with keeping his superior happy, and he develops . . . an elaborate con game. Nobody is interested in real problems of the "outside" world. Rather students are interested in figuring out what the teachers want and trying to give it to them, the teachers do the same with the principals, principals with the superintendents and the superintendents with the school board. . . . [Because very little faith exists between the members of the system], school personnel at every level tend to centralize authority in their own hands. Thus, it becomes natural for the superintendent not to allow his principals to make up their own budgets, for the principals not to allow their teachers to make up their own syllabuses, for the teachers not to allow students to choose their own readings. . . .[2]

2. Harvey Pressman, "New Schools for the Poor," January 1966, mimeographed, p. 15.

This apparent incapacity to reform from within only nourishes rigidity. That rigidity oozes over into shaping the role of the staff and freezing curriculm and instruction.

Administrators and supervisors cannot easily function without risk as agents of change because their role is structured for them to operate as agents of the status quo. The network of rules and checks and balances constructed over the years limits their maneuverability and places a ceiling upon experimentation. A former member of a district school board in New York City saw the heavy hand of the school system at work and concluded:

> The hope for leadership [in the public schools] has been disappointed so often that people have turned in upon themselves, learned to live with meaningless and fantastically detailed rule books, lost any sense of the possibilities outside the narrow structure of the hierarchy of jobs. . . .
>
> Like the former Chinese gentry, New York school administrators are ranked in a rigid hierarchy of status, achieved through the passage of Confucian examinations which fail to measure either the intellectual or temperamental qualities needed for the job.[3]

While principals appear to have a great deal of autonomy, they are, like other civil servants, transfixed by a peculiar double vision; one eye focuses upon pleasing superiors, for advancement in the system goes to those who "play ball with the team"; the other eye focuses on running a tight ship with a minimum of boat rocking from students and teachers, since waves cause trouble. A principal's authority is broad but his primary responsibility is to his superiors.

3. Martin Mayer, "Close to Midnight," *The New York Times,* May 2, 1965.

Subject and area supervisors are also trapped by the system because they are powerless to effect changes and therefore are irrelevant to those they are pledged to help. Teachers need fewer students a day and more contact with them, fewer classes to teach, relief from clerical duties, and more time for planning. Yet, basic as these problems are, supervisors are incapable of resolving them. Supervisors advise, cajole, and persuade principals to make some changes in these areas but they can do little else. Confronted by this powerlessness, supervisors turn inward. They conduct workshops, in-service programs, collect information, visit classes, and prepare sample lesson plans. That an organization can be created with highly paid individuals in responsible positions yet possessing no influence is both ingenious and absurd.

The recent controversy over decentralization in many large urban systems mirrors the lack of confidence some parents and community people have in a centralized bureaucracy possessing the capacity to reform itself. Decentralization, after all, is only a mechanism to redistribute the glob of power concentrated in administrative hands. If that power can be shared by either lower echelon schoolmen or community people or both, then the excess of centralized bureaucracy and monopoly can be curbed and, hopefully, modified. Ultimately, some changes would presumably filter down into the classroom. That's the hope that thrusts parents into picket lines, bars teachers judged inadequate from their classrooms, and catapults the decentralization issue into the headlines.

CURRICULAR RIGOR MORTIS

When one turns to the curriculum, the oppressive drag of inertia is most evident. Furthermore, nowhere is the gap between theory and reality so obvious. Theoreticians conceptualize curriculum as a process of learning influenced by the needs of society and youngsters and, simultaneously, deeply involving those youngsters in its construction and operation. Great. Ask principals and teachers what curriculum is and the answer invariably is a course of study. Content is outlined. Major points are italicized. Activities are suggested. It is what teachers teach and what students take. A detailed syllabus and a textbook make it possible for the student to learn the curriculum. Such a view of curriculum, and it is common enough, adds up to a trunkfull of information that has to be disseminated in slots of equal time 36 weeks a year. School knowledge is viewed as intrinsically valuable and not to be tampered with.

Yet, fundamentally curriculum is a planning and design problem. People—teachers, administrators, experts, the legislator, the community, and, in some cases, students—have to decide what is to be taught. Implementation of the design, again, can be done by curriculum designers in a central office, or by teachers or students. For inner-city schools, the major planning and design time was put in over a half-century ago in most subject areas when schools were serving a little more than half of the nation's children. To be sure changes have taken place in many school districts but, for the most part, the design laid down in the early twentieth century remains in operation in most large urban systems save for the fallout from the Progressive movement in the twenties and thirties which introduced into the curriculum some shallow imitations of John Dewey's ideas. What inner-city students study—the substantive content—save where national curriculum reform efforts have penetrated the ghetto areas—

is pretty much the same as it was for their parents and, in some cases, their grandparents. The youth who graduated (or dropped out) from school before World War I, were it possible for him to return today, would feel very much at home (or alienated) in what teachers would ask him to study. Worse yet, were the teachers who taught at that time to return they could pick up the black roll book and begin lecturing where they had left off and not feel a bit ill at ease.

The point, perhaps overstated, should be clear. A curriculum designed for students years ago is not applicable today. Social studies—that potpourri of history, geography, economics, sociology, *et al.*—will do as an example of obsolescence, inaccuracy, and irrelevancy.[4]

In many inner-city schools, low-income children in elementary schools study the "community." The "community" they study, of course, seldom bears any resemblance to what inner-city kids know and see every day. That one Boston elementary school teacher got a pink slip for teaching Langston Hughes' "Ballad of a Landlord" ("It was not," he was told by the principal, "in the curriculum.") is only a more obvious example. Civics courses in junior high dispense similar pap about Boy-Scout-type communities. In a Kansas City junior high school with a high percentage of poor white and Mexican-American children, I picked up the text-

4. Curriculum reform in social studies, while a late-starter, has been underway since the early 60's. That the movement began outside the schools only underscores the point made earlier about external pressure. But in the case of social studies and other attempts to change curriculum, the money was invested in suburban systems (and college-bound kids) and is just now filtering into "disadvantaged" areas.

book and leafed through while the ninth-grade civics class was watching a film on the cherry blossom festival in Washington, D.C. (Hopefully, the students saw some connection with the chapter they were studying; I didn't). The text had chapter headings like "The School Is a Practice Field for Citizenship" and "A Good Home Is a Small Democracy." Such banalities are insulting to students.

At the fifth, eighth, and eleventh grades, most children take U.S. History. The same machine gun staccato of facts, dates, and useless information confronts youngsters at every step of the way. Worse yet, all the facts aren't there. Stretching to make it from Columbus to Coolidge, few teachers ever reach Pearl Harbor. While more and more texts now carry pictures of Negroes, most teachers are ignorant of multi-ethnic materials; so low-income kids (for that matter, youngsters across the nation) continue to receive the inaccurate white Anglo-Saxon Protestant view of U.S. history. Jonathan Kozol points out that Boston, as late as 1965, still had texts in all-Negro schools that described Africa in the pigmy-cannibal-witch doctor vein. Student protests have pressured administrators to include courses on Negro and African history precisely to counter and eliminate the racism inherent in the curriculum. Distortions and irrelevant information make a mockery out of history; students are dulled by it; militants are outraged; yet teachers teach it.

Some specific examples. In 1963, in the midst of rioting over school integration, one Cleveland teacher pulled down the blinds so her students wouldn't be distracted from her lesson on the Ming dynasty. Or the teachers who religiously used basal readers' series portraying antiseptic suburbs and two-dimensional Mommies and Daddies, because she wanted her class to see the "better" side of life. Or the teacher who continues to perpetuate the myth of Lincoln as the Great Emancipator in the name of giving black youngsters a hero. Or the following class outline given to students in a college-bound class in an all-black high school.

Class Outline for U. S. History

LESSON #1

1. Why did Columbus discover America?
2. Describe the further exploration of the New World?
3. How did the nations of Europe decide on their claims to the New World?

LESSON #2

1. How did each of the major powers settle the New World?
2. Which did you feel was the most lasting form of settlement? Explain why.
   A. Write an essay on your feeling for tomorrow.

LESSON #3

1. What kinds of people came to the English colonies and for what reasons?
2. Describe the settlement of the 13 colonies.

LESSON #4

1. What were the inducements offered to settlers in the English colonies?

LESSON #5

1. Which colony was the birthplace of our democratic system, if any?

DEBATE: Divide class into 13 colonies with a colony to defend.

LESSON #6

1. What effects did the Puritan's religion have on the U.S. in the following areas: A. Education? B. Northern states? C. Towns?

2. Why was there political unrest in some of the English colonies?

3. Why did the Indians like the French and not the English?

LESSON #7

1. What were the causes of the French and Indian War?

2. Winston Churchill said "Wars are won by the mistakes of the enemy." Explain this statement in relation to the French and Indian War.

3. What are the results of the French and Indian War? Do you see any connection with the American Revolution?

LESSON #8

Test on Unit 1

The inaccuracies, distortions, omissions, and triviality—not to mention the repetition—within this outline underscore the irrelevancy of the conventional curriculum for the inner-city youngster.

All of this is to say that a more responsive curriculum has to be designed and implemented. Easier said than done. Curriculum developers point with pride to the logical (to whom?) sequence of content and skills between kindergarten and graduation. Indeed, they have invested much time and energy into slicing off bits of knowledge, packaging it, and presenting it to students as they proceed at the same pace up the ladder of education. One, for example, must go through the first grade before the second; one must study the family before the community; one must take French 1 before French 2. These prepackaged steps have little to do with how kids learn. They are convenient, however, and present a pseudo-efficient stance to non-professionals. The presumptuousness of breaking knowledge down into artificially manageable chunks has been exposed by youngsters who learn to read before school, write poems without any instruction, and compute odds and amounts of money without learning fractions.

Sequential curriculum is given the lie by students, jumped into a higher grade, who perform satisfactorily in spite of having missed earlier courses. Perhaps the best way to illustrate how standardization of curriculum and irrelevance are inherently inadequate is to imagine, as Paul Goodman does, how the schools might teach speaking.

> If we tried to teach children to speak, by academic methods in a school-like environment, many would fail and most would stammer. . . .
>
> 1. Speaking would be a curricular subject abstracted from the web of activity and reserved for special hours punctuated by bells.
>
> 2. It would be a tool subject rather than a way of being in the world.

> 3. It would not spring from his needs in immediate situations but would be taught according to the teacher's idea of his future advantage, importantly aiming at his getting a job sixteen years later.
>
> 4. Therefore the child would have to be "motivated"; the exercises would have to be "fun," etc.
>
> 5. The lessons would be arranged in a graded series from simple to complex, for instance, on a false theory that monosyllables precede polysyllables, or words precede sentences, or sentences precede words.
>
> 6. The teacher's relation to the infant would be further depersonalized by the need to speak or listen to only what fits two dozen other children as well.
>
> 7. Being continually called on, corrected, tested and evaluated to meet a standard in a group, some children would become stutterers; others would devise a phony system of apparently speaking in order to get by, although the speech meant nothing; others would balk at being processed and would purposely become "stupid."
>
> 8. Since there is a predetermined range of what can be spoken and how it must be spoken, everybody's speech would be pedantic and standard, without truth to the child's own experience or feeling.[5]

The well-documented lack of motivation endemic in inner-city schools, as Goodman suggests, is not so much a cause as it is a symptom of irrelevancy, standardization, and pseudo-scientific curriculum development.

INSTRUCTIONAL RIGOR MORTIS

If an obsolete curriculum helps to turn students off, the manner of instruction only shuts them out further. What too

5. Paul Goodman, "Mini-Schools: A Prescription for the Reading Problem," *New York Review of Books,* January 4, 1968, p. 16.

many observers fail to realize is that the content of the curriculum and how it is taught are inseparable. Divorcing the two can only create artificial categories suitable, perhaps, for educators at the college level, but clearly unrelated to what happens in the classroom. Because most view the curriculum as a static body of information, not to be violated, the task of instruction is merely to disseminate information. Thus, lectures, recitation, outlining text chapters, oral reports, answering questions at the end of chapters. Thus, teacher-talk predominates. Thus, pouring in rather than drawing out. Student talk is procedural (Will this be on the test?), disruptive, or covert. Again, the structural situation—i.e., a required, static body of information—dictates how teachers teach. And for teachers of low-income youngsters, for whom classroom control is the problem, curriculum and instruction become additional weapons to establish silence and coerce conformity.

In one classroom I observed, an experienced teacher, a devotee of the new math, was introducing the "less than" and "more than" symbols < > to her second graders. She told the class what each sign meant and gave an example of it. She repeated this procedure three times. At certain points the class chorused back to her what each sign meant, especially after each example. The children answered correctly in unison. Meanwhile, four or five kids were inattentive. The teacher skillfully stared one into silence and swiftly motioned the others to place their heads on their desks, which they did. It was a masterful performance of fingertip classroom control. Finally, an exercise sheet was passed out and the class, save for the children who were reprimanded, industriously attacked the assignment. Later on in the day, I looked at the completed sheets and discovered that over three-quarters of the class did not have the faintest idea of what the symbols meant. I asked her why the results were so poor. She replied, this section of the second grade was the "lowest" and that they were simply unable to comprehend the new math, "It is too difficult for our children." The possibility that telling is not learning or that rote recitation of abstractions is not an effective technique or that the prescribed approach in the teacher's manual was inappropriate was not raised. The introduction of innovative curriculum materials in no way guarantees a departure from the conventional spewing out of facts which is woven into the very fabric of the curriculum.

Middle- and upper-income youngsters forced to endure this content and instruction will survive in spite of the nineteenth century approach. Low-income youngsters smell the irrelevance sooner and act upon it earlier, be they "push outs," students who endure twelve years for the piece of paper, or the ones who openly rebel. All place a high value upon education, but they see the school as meaningless and an absurd waste of time.

What we have, then, in a school system serving large numbers of the ethnic poor is a tangle of pathology. So often a radically isolated, highly bureaucratized institution has jerry-built a network of rules and functions each designed for a specific purpose, but having little to do with teaching and learning. Worse yet, they suffocate initiative and flexibility. Low-income children are at the mercy of a system that traps teachers, administrators, and others into performing roles they do not wish to, into saying things they would not say in other situations, into generally behaving as people who don't care for youngsters. Such a system turns out conforming producers of obsolescent information and educationally scarred rejects, not independent, inquiring youths anxious to live in an ever-changing complex world. "The schools," a writer concluded, "are failing the children; that is why the children are failing in school."[6]

To change children, schools must change.

6. Harvey Pressman, "New Schools for the Poor," January, 1966, mimeographed, p. 9.

Part 2

The Way Things Could Be

If my description of the way things are in inner-city schools is accurate, and the evidence that it is continues to mount, then why write anything on what teachers can do? It is a fair question because the voices of discontent grow even louder as confidence in the schools sinks even lower. Plans for dismembering the public schools—decentralization being the current swing of the pendulum—in effect, turning them over to anyone who is willing to take on the job (parents, business, universities, the military) are discussed seriously.[1] Alternatives that would break the public school's monopoly on education and establish competitive operations ranging from Paul Goodman's mini-schools to state operated classrooms receive open attention from the foundations as well as federal officials.

If the urban public school system is bankrupt, what can matter, do? If the constraints upon teachers and students are an isolated, very vulnerable teacher, or principal, for that so deadening, can any vitality remain, much less survive? My last ounce of faith in public education is invested in positive answers to both questions. As bad as inner-city schools are, effective teaching does occur. In the face of enormous obstacles, contrived and accidental, men and women labor at communicating with youngsters who fundamentally want to learn although many have erected barbed wire fences in their attempt to survive in school. These teachers and administrators unceasingly peel back encrusted layers of apathy, distrust, and boredom to uncover curiosity and stimulate involvement with

1. In recent times the mayor of Jersey City, N.J., offered the public school system to the Ford Foundation. The offer was declined.

ideas and people. There are classrooms and schools where kids really want to learn and do learn. Consider what might happen to education if these teachers and youngsters, and millions more, were given the freedom, surroundings, and training to make it happen. A frail hope, indeed, to hang a book upon. But I do have faith in the value of a public education, albeit an eroding one, and I'm not ready to junk it.

That a frail hope exists in no way diminishes the urgency for overhauling public schools, especially those of the inner-city but not, by any means, limited to them. Systemic changes must be political and educational; they must deal concretely with power relationships and the allocation of resources. Once begun, reforms will ripple outward toward suburbs as some already have done. Unless, and this is the crucial point, the school system does change, equal educational opportunity and quality education (however defined) will remain pieties to be trotted out after the looters have had their fill.

Amidst my skepticism, and well protected from the cynicism that paralyzes involvement, is this belief that a school can make a difference in a child's life and allow that youngster's abilities to surface and develop. While many would agree in principle, some would argue that a bankrupt system prevents productive intervention. Perhaps. But inner-city youngsters cannot afford to have teachers and administrators wait around for changes to happen. No stroke of lightning directive from the Almighty nor penetrating analysis will revamp the schools. Words, contrary to the fantasies of certain critics, will not make public schools disappear. Nor can anyone in this nation afford to wait out the battle on the sidelines or retreat to suburban schools until the system is reformed. It will take much energy and grubby work on the part of politicians, citizens, and educators to begin the long climb upward from the nadir that inner-city schools have sunk to. After all, it took decades of indifference and neglect for them to touch bottom. As the effort proceeds, a generation of school children must be dealt with. They will have to have teachers better than they have had. They have to have curricula that makes sense to them. They will will have to participate more in the learning process. To those moralists among the critics who argue that any accommodation with the system—i.e., preparing teachers, revising curricula, and so on—is evil in that it prolongs the life of the public school system, I can only reply that the kids are going to be in the classrooms for some time whether we like it or not. Ignoring their needs in the hope of the system's eventual collapse may be a fine debate topic for a graduate seminar (e.g., "The Pros and Cons of Non-Cooperation") but I'm much more concerned over what happens to children today and tomorrow and my capacity to alter those events.

Fortunately, there are teachers who deal with children imaginatively; they can make a difference. Yet one of them, Herbert Kohl, describes in *36 Children* how he left the classroom finally and afterward saw the promise erode in many of his former pupils. He concludes that it was cruel and even a waste of time to give youngsters one good year. Quite often effective teachers torture themselves with such thoughts. They are tired, but short-sighted, I feel. The long view is that one year is better than none; one capable teacher is better than a hack occupying classroom space. If there were five or seven more like-minded teachers in Kohl's school, perhaps he would have stayed. There are Kohls scattered throughout the inner-city of every city as assuredly as there are imaginative principals. The problem, at least one of the problems, is how to increase their numbers and find the means to support their efforts with able administrators while the struggle for reforms continues at different levels.

Different models of effective classroom teaching, flexible and still viable in the face of suffocating obstacles, have been developed and implemented. More must be developed. As the pressure upon school systems to reform mounts, rigidity will melt. As decentralization plans are executed, more and more opportunities for experimentation will appear. Those models of teaching that have proved themselves effective amidst the mind-boggling conformity of inner-city schools will offer extraordinary openings for broader use when the cobwebs are wiped away and the structure loosened up sufficiently for principals, teachers, and students to operate more freely. Thus, I'm concerned about a very small niche of the debate on inner-city schools: What are some effective teaching methods?[2]

THE CARDOZO PROJECT IN URBAN TEACHING

One model that has worked under the most trying of battlefield conditions—the inner-city classroom—has emerged, scarred but still functioning, and most important, still possessing the adaptability—once constraints are eliminated—to penetrate diverse teaching situations. The ingredients, none

2. I assume that an effective teaching model for inner-city youngsters also applies to suburban classrooms; the reverse, however, is not applicable.

of which is unique, grow out of my own classroom experiences, extensive observations of schools in various parts of the country, and four years as a member of the Cardozo Project in Urban Teaching. Since this program was one of the chief models for the design of the legislation and operation of the national Teacher Corps, a brief description is in order.

Begun in 1963 as a pilot project at Cardozo High School in Washington, D.C., the program recruited ten returned Peace Corps volunteers as intern teachers in the areas of social studies and English. In the next four years, seventy-five returning PCV's, recent college graduates, housewives—anyone with a B.A. degree with or without prior educational training—interned as teachers in an elementary school, junior high school, or senior high school. The program linked initially to Howard University, later to include Antioch and Trinity (D.C.) college, offered a M.A.T. degree after completion of the internship.

The program, focusing upon classroom teaching, was divided into four parts: supervised internship, seminars, development of curriculum materials, and contact with students and community.

During his internship, each trainee taught two classes in the junior or senior high school or a half-day at the elementary level from September to June under the close supervision of curriculum specialists who also taught (the ratio of specialist to interns was roughly 1:5). The classroom became a laboratory for instruction and experimentation. Interns have agreed that this empahsis on actual classroom teaching combined with complete accessibility to a master practitioner has been the main strength of the project.

In a real sense, the seeds of success or failure for this

phase of the program rested upon the curriculum specialist. He had to have extensive classroom experience, familiarity with current curricular innovations, and a firm grounding in subject matter and methodology. Most important, the specialist had to be open-minded toward classroom teaching (i.e., while we know some things that will work in conventionally organized teaching situations, there is much we don't know about what happens in a classroom, about youngsters, and about ourselves). Thus, an open style of inquiry married to a knowledge of existing theory and practice unite within the specialist. Rather than continue to define the role in abstract terms, let a former intern describe what happened between herself and one master teacher (a term then used interchangeably with curriculum specialist).

> What goes on in dialogue (between intern and master teacher) is extremely difficult to describe but the continuity, frankness, humor and concern which the master teachers bring to their jobs constantly engage the intern in meaningful evaluation, questioning and understanding. The fact that the master teacher is also in the classroom is infinitely important, for not only does the intern benefit from observation of the master teacher, but the master teacher can evaluate the successes and failures, problems and strengths of the intern not only in terms of what he knows and observes of the intern, but also in terms of what he knows and understands of the kids in school. The master teacher is also there constantly when the impression of the difficult session, the misfired lesson, the glorious success is fresh and full. That is the time for evaluation and understanding even if the master teacher has not been in the classroom for that class.
>
> Another advantage of the closeness between intern and master teacher has to do directly with the subject matter. . . . Not only does the master teacher suggest directions and

> specific materials in terms of books, units and extensions of materials already presented, but the master teacher has unique perspective to evaluate and develop ideas and implications from material which is successful or unsuccessful in the intern's classroom.[3]

The purpose of the supervised internship was to arm trainees with a realistic repertoire of knowledge and skills that would work with youngsters in inner-city classrooms but, most important, also to equip them with questions that effective teachers must constantly ask of themselves regardless of the particular classroom. Asking the right questions, we felt, was far more useful to new teachers than programing them with pat answers for "typical" situations. After nine months of classroom training where they exercised responsibility under close supervision, those questions were internalized and continually asked when they entered their own classrooms as full-time teachers.

The second phase of the program involved after-school seminars. Interns, staff, and interested faculty members of the participating schools met several afternoons a week at the high school to investigate the sociology of urban life, the psychological disciplines, humanities, and the methods of teaching English, social studies, math, and the elementary subjects. Graduate credit for these seminars and the internship led, over a two-year period, to the Master of Arts in Teaching degree.

Since the staff felt strongly that the teacher-training curriculum should be a useful tool to the trainees, growing out of their needs and concerns rather than imposed by the staff

3. From evaluation of program by Mrs. Carolyn Wylie, English intern, 1963–64.

or university, certain seminars appeared and disappeared over the years I was involved with the program. The ones mentioned above, for the most part, constituted the curriculum for interns. In 1966–67, for example, the year-long seminars were in humanities, methods, and curriculum materials development, with the urban sociology and psychological disciplines offerings being taught in the summer prior to the supervised internship.

A brief word on these seminars. Urban sociology concentrated on the relationship between school and community. What is the city like? How did the urban school become what it is? Inevitably, discussion turned toward the dynamics of power and powerlessness in the city and the schools and their effects upon the curriculum and the student. The psychological disciplines seminar investigated the role of the teacher in the inner-city schools and the diversity of behavior among low-income youngsters. Clinical approaches to youngsters and self-evaluation as a teacher also were pursued in these sessions. The methods seminars, taught in most cases by the master teachers, focused upon problems arising from the day-to-day classroom experiences which, ultimately, led to the larger questions of what to teach and how it should be taught. The humanities seminar pursued the themes of growing up, the city, education, and the school as seen through the eyes of writers of fiction and non-fiction. Readings were drawn from Margaret Mead's *Growing Up in Samoa,* Edgar Friedenburg's *Vanishing Adolescent,* Paul Goodman's *Growing Up Absurd,* Richard Wright's *Black Boy,* Jane Jacob's *Life and Death of Great Cities,* John Holt's *How Children Fail,* and others.

All these seminars had three points in common:

1. To a great extent, content for seminars emerged out of the interns' experiences. Modifications, deletions, and additions occurred whenever the group's need was expressed with certainty and unanimity.

2. Discussions were firmly grounded in the reality of the classrooms. Saccharine platitudes and wishful idealism, far removed from reality, were quickly—often mercilessly—torn apart by interns and staff.

3. Educators, psychologists, community workers, sociologists—local and national—each exploring the frontiers of their interest, shared their ideas with us.

One intern described the seminars this way.

> The continual discussion about subject matter, English for me, psychology, sociology and educational philosophy is not confusing or without discipline because we always are building around the focal point of our experience in class. When I am told that all kids can learn or that all kids are stupid I can test these assertions against my experience. When I think about the meaning of a poem, I think how it would be meaningful to my class. When I hear about the psychology of adolescent development, I can think about my students and not an abstract, lifeless body of people who fit under the label of adolescents. When I discuss sociological descriptions of the urban scene, I think of how these statistics, generalizations and theories can create over-simplified paper people. The real teaching situation unites knowledge and experience from usually separated sources, not only making the class more interesting, but also giving a significant bond to the varied material.[4]

Development of curriculum materials was the third phase of the program. The assumption was that what had been

4. From evaluation of program by Tom Wilson, intern 1963–64.

used with youngsters—i.e., textbooks, workbooks, and the like —had failed to generate sufficient enthusiasm to learn and achieve. Different materials had to be found and created to engage youngsters. Throughout the year, materials developed by staff and former interns in addition to materials commercially produced were available to the trainees. During the second semester, a seminar on the development of materials was led by the master teacher. Interns were expected to produce lessons and units of their own that could be tried out in their classrooms. While we were concerned with producing actual instructional materials and using them in class, we were more interested in the process of creating materials—i.e., asking one's self: What do I want to teach? Why did I want to teach it? How do I know I've taught it? and so on. The program also advanced $100 to each intern for purchasing curriculum materials, again to prod each person to ask questions about the purposes and uses of the material before he purchased it and used it in class. Such an approach placed full faith in intelligent adults to make professional judgments about what and how to teach.

The last phase of the program involved contact with students and the community. Here the assumption was that decisions on how and what to teach had to be based upon some knowledge of youngsters and their environments. To achieve this, a number of different tactics were used. One year, interns were assigned to neighborhood anti-poverty centers one day a week for three months; another year, an intensive two-week summer program concentrating upon individual and community contacts was held. Whichever approach, a sizeable block of time remained each school year for interns to get to know their youngsters and the community in any way they chose. The results, as expected, varied widely. Since the focus of the program was upon becoming effective classroom teachers, the information gained was instrumental in interns making referrals, choosing materials, and assisting individual youngsters; the community was another instructional resource, and a crucial one, that had to be utilized by anyone teaching in inner-city classrooms.

The Cardozo Project in Urban Teaching, as described here, was judged successful by an independent evaluation and by the school officials of the District of Columbia, who decided to budget funds for its incorporation (now called the Urban Teacher Corps) into the regular program and expand its operation. All of this is not to say that this model of training and teaching was free of problems (it wasn't) or that the project solved some of the serious ills confronting public school education (it didn't); it was, however, one of those first steps in the thousand-mile journey that the public schools have to take, in this instance, to attract and train young men and women who would not ordinarily go into an inner-city classroom.

I've described the program in some detail because it contained most of the ingredients for effective teaching. The model of the teacher emerging from the project was that of a multi-faceted decision-maker: a classroom teacher with a sharply reduced load, a developer of instructional materials, and a liaison with student and community. Each facet of this model will be discussed in the next three chapters.

Chapter IV

Developing Curriculum Materials

Readers eagerly expecting recipes for "success" and revelations of innovative techniques to apply will be sorely disappointed in the next three chapters. Surely to those who are preparing to teach but fear for the future or to those who have become disillusioned with the classroom and are grasping for easy answers or to frustrated laymen irritated over urban school decay and anxious for solution —surely they must know that words are inefficient tools for allaying fears or shaping behavior.[1]

1. I doubt very much whether telling people something and ex-

Furthermore, readers will be disappointed if they believe teaching involves mechanically applying formulas laid down by "experts," lifting successful techniques from others, or just loving kids. No book, least of all this one, can tell anyone how to teach. The skills, attitudes, and knowledge necessary to teach effectively in the inner-city are best learned in the schools themselves under the guidance of crack master teachers and university-affiliated clinical professors, who also teach. What a book like this can do is to lay out some guidelines, some hunches on what should be done in and out of the classroom with appropriate explanations. Although I lack the pedagogical preparation in supervision and curriculum development, I make no apologies for the conclusions; what I or other practitioners have to say will make some sense or none at all only when measured against what happens in the classroom.

Mention curriculum and students shrink, teachers clear their throats to lecture, and principals pull out courses of study from their desks. The word causes knee-jerk reactions from each and all. And that's to be expected. After all, curriculum is considered by many to be what a school teaches and what children are expected to learn; it is textbooks, basal readers, syllabi, and course outlines. It is the school's slice of reality. The Board of Education, the superintendent, principals, and special interest groups determine that reality. Teachers teach it. Kids endure it. That's all.

---

pecting behavioral change ever really happens—unless coercion is applied. Teaching, like most other professions, with its theory, skills, knowledge, and styles of operation is, I feel, best learned in actual participation under competent supervision. While words may be inefficient they need not be ineffectual especially if they are placed in the hands of individuals who want change.

The curriculum in inner-city schools is a huge glob of undigested facts that is smoothed out like peanut butter and spooned to captive students nine months a year for twelve consecutive years, four more for those who choose college. Teachers package and disseminate the knowledge; students are supposed to digest it and become productive citizens.[2] Like peanut butter, sometimes it sticks in the throat. Knowing information becomes the operational, though unstated, objective of the curriculum. Knowledge is seen as intrinsically good. And in case some don't get the message, grades, achievement tests, and ability grouping lock kids into sitting and listening for the bulk of their waking time in school, thereby getting the medium across. "Well," a young honors student said in an interview a few years ago, "curriculum is curriculum. We have it for twelve years. We haven't mentioned it because we wanted to tell you about the things that really matter."[3]

Why is this? The answer is that the curriculum is the only tangible evidence that the school is trying to fulfill the aims of education. Those noble aims—social commitment to democratic ideals, respect for the traditions and values of our culture, and so forth—are reduced by schoolmen to an enor-

2. Then there is the hidden curriculum. What students learn and teach one another in the halls, gyms, cafeterias, auditorium, and toilets about the latest dress, dance steps, language, and mores of the age comprise these learning experiences. And this curriculum is reality for the kids. No Board of Education, superintendent, principal, or special interest group, and certainly no teacher, decides the content of this informal curriculum. It belongs wholly to the kids. And none of it ever gets into the classroom.

3. David Mallery, *High School Students Speak Out* (Harper and Row, 1962), p. 17.

mous array of facts and isolated chunks of information. Like monumental statuary, the curriculum stands as testimony to the goals of education.

Stated crudely, the assumption underpinning the curriculum is that knowing certain information and skills will get kids jobs or into college. "Learn this," so many teachers say in word and deed, "if you want to get a job." Knowing information as opposed to an operational understanding of concepts and generalizations becomes an end in itself. Dr. Mark Krug, a professor of education and history at the University of Chicago, unabashedly put it this way:

> Is it or is it not important for high school graduates and college freshmen to know about the Populist Rebellion, the War of 1812, about Daniel Webster and Marcy Tweed, about the Clay Compromise, about the Teapot Dome Scandal . . .? Is it or is it not important for high school graduates to know about Caesar, the Carthaginian Wars, about Constantine, about Ghengis Khan, the reforms of Ahkbar and the wisdom of Confucius, about Voltaire, Napoleon and Waterloo? The assumption postulated here is that such—and similarly related knowledge . . . is essential and worthwhile in any moderately educated man. I would shudder to think that a college freshman would have to see a Broadway play to become acquainted for the first time with the woman of Troy, the complicated nature of Marat or the tragic downfall of Charles Dilke.[4]

While Krug's quote begs for response, I'll let it stand as evidence that some believe that the job of curriculum and instruction is to pack kids with "important" facts in order to

4. Mark Krug, "Bruner's New Social Studies: A Critique" *Social Education,* October, 1966, p. 405.

produce solid, middle-class, educated citizens. Thus, the function of the curriculum is to distill global aims into a series of experiences that will result in certain types of children. In other words, when someone asks why adopt this curriculum rather than another, the answer hinges upon the kinds of kids you want to emerge from schools.

IDEAL AIMS OF THE CURRICULUM

Read, for example, the following aims of an inner-city high school in a large eastern seaboard city. (This is taken from a handbook for parents.)

> The process of education with which the school is concerned is the development of the individual to his fullest potential. Each has the right to secure through an educational system the type of experience which will develop personal, vocational, social and cultural competencies needed in our society. However, education is not only a right and privilege [sic], it is also a necessity to both our nation and to the individual if both are to survive.
>
> The school must accept the responsibility for solving problems created by the effects of technology and science on society. It must increase its holding power through experimentation with new methods and through provision of widely varying curriculums to meet the needs of the individual in a world of rapid change. . . .
>
> With these facts [sic] in mind, we have formulated the following objectives:
>
> - To provide the best possible academic education for pupils to benefit—with emphasis on counseling and testing; grouping according to abilities; needs and interest; experimentation; and tutorial services.

- To satisfy needs for occupational training and individual and group counseling; through provision of work-study programs, assistance in job placement, . . .
- To develop through appropriate activities an appreciation of our culture and its aesthetic values and an interest in other cultures of the world.
- To inculcate, through a vigorous health program, attitudes and habits which will enhance physical well-being and good sportsmanship.
- To instill through classroom and extra-curricular activities some feeling of individual worth which the student will carry over into his relationship with others. . . .
- To evaluate the curriculum constantly through follow-up of graduates and former . . . students so that the program of studies might be a more effective instrument in education.
- To include students in the planning necessary for organized school life so that these young people will experience self-discipline, self-government and responsibility. . . .
- To involve parents in helping to plan for the growth and development of their children.

Now, note the courses of study available to students.

REQUIREMENTS FOR GRADUATION BY TRACK SEQUENCE

In each curriculum, a total of 16 Carnegie units, plus physical education, is required for graduation.

Track I—Honors

Placement in this track is available to students who have demonstrated ability to do advanced work and have shown a valid interest in accelerated placement. Parents or guardians must approve such placement.

Subjects	*Units*	
English	4	Physical Education
Foreign Languages	2	Cadets (a military
Mathematics	2	training course)
Science	2	required unless ex-
Social Studies	2	cused
Total:	12	

At least two additional units must be selected from the following fields:

English
Mathematics
Science
Foreign Languages
Social Studies

Track II—College Preparatory

Placement in this track is based upon the student's preparation and evidence of his ability to do the calibre of work in English, mathematics, science and the foreign languages required for college entrance.

Subjects	*Units*	
English	4	Physical Education
Foreign Languages	2	Cadets
Mathematics	2	
Science	1	
Social Studies	1½	
Total	10½	

Electives may be selected from the following:

Speech
Advanced Composition
Journalism
Foreign Language
Advanced Mathematics
General Science
Physics
Biology
Chemistry
Social Studies
Art
Industrial Arts

Homemaking	Music
Business Education	Driver Education

Track III—General (Terminal)

Placement in this track is available to students who have demonstrated average ability in reading and in mathematics, who wish a choice of elective subjects, and who plan a terminal program.

Subjects	*Units*	
English	4	Physical Education
Mathematics	1	Cadets
Science	1	
Social Studies	1½	
Total:	7½	

Electives may be selected from the following:

English	Social Studies	Driver Education
Mathematics	Foreign Languages	Homemaking
Science	Industrial Arts	Music
Art	Business Education	

Track IV—Basic (Remedial)

Placement in this track is available to students who have demonstrated average ability in reading and in mathematics, who wish a choice of elective subjects, and who plan a terminal program.

Subjects	*Units*	
English	4	Physical Education
Arithmetic	1	Cadets
Business Practice	1	
Science	1	
Social Studies	2½	
Total:	9½	

Electives may be selected from the following:

Authorized work experience (up to six units)
Art
Industrial Arts
Music
Homemaking
Driver Education

Listing the courses and tracks (which since has been abolished by court order although the streams informally remain) does not give the flavor of the specific content of instruction. Re-read the outline of content on pp. 61–62 and the profile of Mr. Brown on pp. 26–31 for a taste of it. By and large, instruction in each of the subjects is heavily information based, involving at least three-quarters of the teacher's time in talking at kids each forty-minute period. Add the extensive apparatus of tests and ability groupings, and the curriculum functions as a huge collator, sorting out kids to respective occupational slots, most of which have little to do with the abilities of that particular child. The gap between paper and practice verify the real, not the ideal, aims of the curriculum. While the sources of recent student protest are varied, the demand for courses in black history, African cultures, and the like, only reveal a narrow slice of the immense dissatisfaction students feel over what and how they are forced to learn.

It is kind of unfair to continue jabbing at curriculum. Others have done it more eloquently and, I think, more scathingly. (See, for example, the "Phoney School" in Mario Fantini and Gerald Weinstein, *The Disadvantaged* (Harper and Row, 1968).) Let me, instead, deal with some specific issues.

First, my use of the word "curriculum." By curriculum, I should add, I refer to the basic building blocks—lessons and units—more precisely, *curriculum materials* and not the courses of study that constitute a curriculum, say, the honors or basic track, pp. 88–89. A biology course, for example, is taught over a period of 180 days or, roughly—subtracting for tests, assemblies, and days missed—about 150 daily lessons grouped into about eight or ten units. This is the biology course. That it often follows the organization of a textbook only further binds the content of lessons and units to what publishers produce. At the elementary level, a teacher has a syllabus for the school year in each of the content areas or a series of books to cover in a given period of time. The syllabus or books or both are divided into units which break down into daily lessons. My concern is what teachers can do with these building blocks since upon them courses and curricula are built.

I'm concerned with curriculum at this level because the classroom is the place where global objectives and syllabi must be translated into specifics. And the translator is the teacher; his translation is the daily lesson and the larger units he uses, be they of his own creation or in a book. The teacher decides whether to use a basal reader exactly as the manual calls for or to diverge from it or to toss it aside; he decides whether to use the text or a paperback; a film or a workbook exercise. He decides whether facts or concepts should be emphasized and he decides which information should be taught. A crude form of decision-making exists but it must be improved.

Next, curriculum and instruction. As I see them, they are inseparable; the aims of one must be the aims of the other.

Separating the two, as some academicians love to do, is only tearing down straw men. The dichotomy between method and content exists only for those who are ignorant of the teaching process. The aims of the curriculum inevitably shape the content and style of instruction and, conversely, instruction can shape the direction of the curriculum.

A clear example of this can be seen in one teacher's perceptive analysis of language in an inner-city classroom; building on that analysis, she suggests a curriculum which really matches instructional techniques with materials and the teacher's personality. Consider "Bulljive—Language Teaching in a Harlem School" by Gloria Channon.[5]

> Thomas, the third grader who could not make sense of reading, began bringing me samples of his English. . . .
> One day he brought me the word *bullji,* defining it in his usual circumstantial circuitous way: "Somebody is showing you something, how great it is and you say, 'Bullji!' "
>
> I repeated the word as I wrote it down for him: "bull-jive." But here Thomas was on his own territory. He was teaching me. Firmly but politely he rejected my *jive.* "No, no. I said 'bullji.' "
>
> In this instance his ear was more accurate than mine. He was hearing and pronouncing the word exactly as it was in his world. My automatic correction in terms of past experience was quite likely correct. But so was his hearing of the spoken word. . . .
>
> The child operates in the same way. When I say, very distinctly, "I am going to read to you," he files the remark in his language-meaning-category, *I am going to = Amana;* and he responds to it. When I say, "He runs," he hears his version of it, minus the *s.* When I say "most of the time," he hears his word, *mos'.* Conversation and understanding are

5. *Urban Review,* February, 1968, pp. 5–12.

possible between us. By the same token, if the child said to me, "The man jump through the window," I would hear *jumped* and respond to this meaning; "And then what happened?" My machinery for hearing language would be on automatic pilot. I would be listening for meaning.

But sometimes I listen for sounds.

Picture a lesson in rhyming words, a very useful lesson which occurs frequently in the early grades. I write the word *old* on the board. I ask a child to say it. "Ole," he says. "That's right, old. Now give me some words that rhyme with it." "Tole." I know my children don't mean *toll,* so I say "Good," and I write *told* on the board. "Fole?" I record *fold.* "Bole?" "Use it in a sentence." If he should say, "The soldier is bole," I will write it. If he should say, "Bole of cereal," I will reject it. . . . "Pole" is refused. . . . "Role?" Never. I am beginning to be just a little impatient. Why are they so irritatingly erratic in their responses? The child, sensing my tension, is getting worried. Why do I respond so erratically to his words? His faith in himself is shaken. Perhaps I am not after what he thought I wanted. Rhymes for *ole.* Now he will often give up and I will be unable to elicit another word from him. I assume he has run through his meagre vocabulary and feels frustration and despair. . . .

I say, "All right, children. Now, who will read the list we have? And then we will copy it in our notebooks."

A child recites: "Ole, cole, bole, tole, fole. . . ."

It took me a long time to understand why the children in the ghetto classroom would be willing to spend so much time copying anything at all into their books. Children who could not sit still for five minutes in a spoken lesson would sit for a half hour turning out the neatest, most meaningless busywork.

But notice what had been happening. We had a lesson full of misunderstanding and mounting tension. It was a totally irrational session. Neither I nor the children (most of them) could figure out what was going wrong. When we gave up and I asked them to write, the atmosphere began to change. I could walk around the room and admire them for neatness. I could feel a little of the burden of failure lifted from me. They could relax in the glow of approval they were finally earning. . . . For the moment we were free to love each other. But they had become a little more uncertain about their own ability to think, and a little more dependent on me. . . .

A few days ago a child read the sentence: *The girl ran through the meadow.* He defined *meadow,* characteristically, by getting up and tapping the handle of the closet door.

There, in that incident, lies the whole problem:

The phonological one, in which the child perceives *meadow, metal* and *medal* as homonyms;

The lexical one, in which the child does not know the meaning of the word spelled *meadow,* however he pronounces it;

The syntactical one, in which the clues of subject, verb and preposition are ignored in reading, and so all chance of comprehension is lost;

The attitudinal one, where the child accepts that most of his activity in school will be totally and hopelessly meaningless, and that there is no point in his trying to do anything about it, either by questioning himself or his teacher.

Any curriculum designed for teaching such a child must take all four aspects of the problem into account:

Phonological: From the beginning, the teacher must be tuned in to the differences in standard and nonstandard speech. She will then be better able to clarify and correct confusions which arise as a result of them. The child, through observation and imitation, should develop his awareness of the difference in a meaningful and not prejudicial way. From first grade on, reading and spelling should be taught for maximum efficiency, to help the child to hear, read, and spell those of his patterns at greatest variance with standard pronunciations.

Lexical: Through pictures, materials, films and tapes, and most of all through conversations, the child must be helped to label his world. And this world includes the parts of the school world that are alien to him—and every child—the language of fairy tales, for example. Publishers might do well to footnote their stories profusely, as they do when the language is as unfamiliar as Chaucer's or Shakespeare's English. They might well print their stories in natural phrasing patterns rather than fixed margins and continuous lines. . . .

Syntactical: Pattern practice is a must, from Pre-K on. Expansion, the technique which parents use when they converse with their babbling infants, should be used constantly. The child's physical, expressive language must be translated into sentences. We must pick his brain, item by item, for all the ideas hidden in the over-simple verbalizations (*I seen the car*). He must hear and see and *value* his own thoughts expressed in words. He must be exposed to the sounds of standard English, if not in socially and economically integrated schools, then at least through tapes and records of his reading materials. . . .

Attitudinal: That's the tough one. We teachers must change our attitudes and our classroom techniques. We must discard our prejudicial correlation of intelligence with verbal ability and our self-serving assumption that we are teaching when the children are, demonstrably, not learning—no matter how hard we know we are working at our jobs.

Perhaps we may then hope that the child will begin to perceive structure where before he endured chaos, and an active sympathetic intelligence where before he saw a bleak and confusing authority. Only then may he be freed to inquire and to explore and to think and to learn.

Clearly, although Channon is describing a language curriculum, she details instruction, attitudes of the teacher, materials to use, and some goals for that curriculum. The unity of curriculum and instruction cannot be avoided; nor should the aims of curriculum be avoided.

SOME REAL AIMS OF CURRICULUM MATERIALS

For curriculum materials or, for that matter, a course of study, a workshop, a college—for any instrument of education—there are three possible aims: to have students know information, concepts and generalizations; to have students develop certain attitudes; and to have students able to perform particular skills. Although these categories overlap, it is possible, indeed probable, that all three or two or one can be aims, depending upon what the curriculum developer decides he wants to teach. What every teacher is after, of course, is the behavioral change that each objective implies.

I've already suggested that knowledge for its own sake as a prime objective, especially in imparting specific bits of information, fails simply because of the fantastic multiplication of knowledge occurring every year. Additionally, knowledge as delivered in the traditional packages has hardened and become irrelevant to what youngsters see as reality. Should, for example, *Hamlet* be taught because it is part of the western tradition and all youngsters growing up in that culture should have a crack at the Prince of Denmark if for no other reason than exposure and appreciation? Or should it be taught to connect the concepts of universality and timelessness of man's conflict with himself and his environment with the student's life while simultaneously developing a wide repertoire of thinking, writing, and oral skills? No to the first question and yes to the second. Notice that the reasons I gave for each position on *Hamlet* suggest alternative teaching strategies—i.e., if I were teaching so that students would know and appreciate Shakespeare, I would present the play differently from the way I would were I teaching for concepts and skill development. And this brings me to my third point.

Functionally, curriculum materials are tools and limited ones at that; they are not products to consume. As with any tool, they are used to achieve particular aims, be they knowledge, skills, or attitudes. To conceive of lessons and units as instruments broadens the dialogue to include discussion over what kinds of people the schools are to produce—the fundamental question of all education. Toward what ends should curriculum materials and instruction be turned?

My answer is brief. I want kids to be able to, in Paul Woodring's words, "make wise decisions." To me, in a free society individuals must be equipped with those mental and social skills and functional knowledge necessary to make choices in coping with a constantly changing environment. Skill development is the priority; knowledge is the vehicle to develop and improve mental abilities and academic and interpersonal skills. While such a goal is worthwhile for all children, it is essential for inner-city youngsters who are threatened, on the one hand, by those who don't care and, on the other, by elitists who, wanting the poor to be the vanguard of massive educational change, wish to drown them in compassion, culture, and experiments.

Do not construe my point as anti-intellectual or as a plea for "life adjustment" or strict vocational preparation; it is, I feel, a recognition that the life span of school-produced knowledge is brief and often perceived as worthless by kids. We just cannot predict what information will be useful to children a generation from now, much less a decade hence. We can, however, estimate with a degree of certainty that a person must have minimum academic skills, developed mental abilities to make judgments on public and private issues, and interpersonal skills necessary to negotiate the complex, industrial society we live in.

Such a view does not mean Shakespeare automatically vanishes from the curriculum; it does suggest that humanists had better get themselves together and shake out some cobwebs or he may well disappear. History doesn't have to die, although what is called history by school people and its manner of instruction deserve interment. The traditional reasons for Columbus, *Silas Marner,* and the Linnaean classification system demand re-examination. No longer are the clients of this form of knowledge going to be satisfied with "you'll need it later" or "it's important to know." The rationale for curriculum materials must deal with the broad range of skills kids need to perform effectively once formal education ends, and the concepts and principles necessary for them to understand the dynamics of what is happening around them.

What about attitudes? Shouldn't materials teach attitudes like respect for democratic values, morality, patriotism, improved self-image, and the like? Aren't these valid aims of education and therefore appropriate for curriculum materials? Read the aims of the reform-minded Greater Cleveland Social Science Program for a sequential curriculum between kindergarten and twelfth grade. "The program," a brochure states, "stresses the American heritage of freedom; it develops respect for human dignity; it instills the sense of social responsibility and it tries to inculcate a spirit of life-long interest in the welfare of the community, state, nation, and mankind."

These and similar statements may be valid aims but I doubt seriously if attitudinal changes (which anticipate and shape behavioral change) such as developing respect for human dignity and instilling a sense of social responsibility ever really occur as a result of curriculum materials. That an inherent conflict emerges between the development of inquiry and analysis and the inculcation of certain values only reflects the complexity of education. To clarify values, especially when they clash, is very different from instilling them. It is the difference between developing materials around the question: Are property rights more important than human rights? or creating materials that convey the point that looters are destructive to the social fabric of America and therefore should be dealt with harshly. Perhaps I can make the point about attitudes and their use as direct teaching aims by examining the current interest in Negro history and multi-ethnic materials.

LINKING REAL AIMS WITH REAL MATERIALS: NEGRO HISTORY

To the historians and teachers who have labored long and hard to correct the distorted picture of the black American's experiences in texts and in classrooms, the deluge of curriculum materials (units, paperbacks, textbooks) fell upon parched lips. So little had happened previously, now so much. Congressional investigations of bias in textbooks, state laws prohibiting prejudicial treatment of minorites in materials, and school boards mandating the teaching of Negro history testify to the interest and concern of black and white Americans in the issue.

Yet to examine the aims of the materials that have been produced by publishers, school systems, and private individuals raises some serious questions about their limitations and use in the classroom.

There seem to be three main objectives for the development of materials on the Negro:

1. To offer white and black students a more balanced picture of the American past than has been previously presented. This aim embraces the attempt to remove the crude stereotypes and ugly phraseology that marred many texts, films, and other teaching materials and to fill in the obvious gaps of information that existed.

2. To improve interracial relations. The assumption is that once, accurate information is learned, intergroup tensions —some of which are based upon ignorance—will be reduced.

3. To improve the self-concept of black children. Here, the belief is that how a youngster sees himself determines his behavior. Since black children, especially poor ones, have a negative picture of themselves—according to this view— instructional materials stressing racial illustrations and achievements of the race will increase self-esteem, instill pride, and ultimately produce socialy acceptable behavior.

The first aim calls for information on the role of the Negro in American life; kids are asked to know facts for the simple reason that hitherto they have been omitted or whitewashed. The second and third aims suggest that once kids know these facts attitudinal and behavioral changes will occur. These latter aims disturb me. The basic question is whether studying Negro history will improve self-concept and instill pride. The only answer now has to be: No one knows. No research evidence has been produced to demonstrate whether kids will see themselves and their race in a more favorable light as a result of a book, instructional materials, or a course in school. That no evidence exists, of course, does not mean increased self-esteem and pride aren't produced; absence of evidence may be due to imprecise instruments, inferior methodology, or gutless researchers. Whatever the reason, having Benjamin Banneker or Nat Turner on bulletin boards or in primers for little black boys and girls may warm the hearts of liberals and activists, but it will not have any measurable effect in changing how a child sees himself and how he acts.

Part of the problem is the concept of the self-image. Many view it as a muscle that can be kneaded, nourished, and exercised into a full performance. As I understand it and from my own experiences, I am pretty sure that it is a complex multi-dimensional set of perceptions about one's self jerry-built over the years from experiences. Thus, a kid who has low esteem academically may be the first chosen on the street basketball court or the most respected pool player. He thinks well of himself in some areas, less so in others. But because academic success is so highly valued, such youngsters are judged to have a low self-concept. This assumption—a one-dimensional self-concept—forms the rationale for creating a course or writing a book for the express purpose of instilling pride and enhancing self-image. Such efforts inflate the value of words far beyond their capacity to deliver.

Another reason for my concern about teaching attitudes directly is that excessive good-will and compassion on the part of teachers, historians, and publishers will undermine effective history teaching. Consider what one respected educator has urged:

> The Negro child, from the earliest school entry through graduation from high school needs continued opportunities to see himself and his racial group in a realistically positive light.[6]

While most would approve of the sentiment behind this statement, such a view has serious implications. To show a group of people in a "realistically positive light" places, I feel, too high a premium on selection of achievements and success and ignores analyses of failures and setbacks. Selecting materials that will have youngsters think well of themselves (and, remember, we don't know if they will) implies a manipulative use of historical sources to obtain a so-called desirable end. Selecting only the hero, only the victory, only the success story presents the positive side of history; it is propaganda. I don't know if it works, but I do know that its place is in the storefront, not the classroom; its teacher is the true believer, not an inquirer, and it can only be taught by a race-conscious black man, not a white man. Angry activists would argue that white propaganda and white mythology have been taught in the schools for decades; now it's time for a darker brand. Based upon the sorry record of what has been taught, there is justice to the demand but inherent in this argument is the view of the student as a passive absorber of the "proper" information. I and others would see the student as an active inquirer evaluating, analyzing, and judging attitudes, values, and knowledge. White and black activists ironically practice a perverse paternalism by subtly reinforcing the myth that the Negro possesses limited intel-

6. William C. Kvaraceus, *et al., Negro Self-Concept* (New York: McGraw-Hill, 1965), p. 21.

lectual ability and, therefore, cannot decide for himself what is true or false. The propagandist, be he white or black, doesn't really trust kids to learn the "truth." It must be told to them. And this raises the last problem.

In the recent sweep of curricular reform in the social studies, the accumulation of factual knowledge has *not* been of primary importance. Far more emphasis has been placed upon developing the skills of comprehension, evaluation, and analysis. Such an emphasis runs counter to the aim of developing a positive self-concept through instructional materials. Consider a unit on the city. When the unit turns to the ghetto (and I cannot conceive of any urban social studies teacher ignoring the ghetto) how can we examine the social, economic, and political factors that create and sustain a slum in a "realistically positive light"? Are we to dwell only on the Althea Gibsons, Claude Browns, and James Baldwins who clawed their ways out of the crippling pathology or are we to have the students analyze the anatomy of the ghetto and society that permits a trickle to escape while condemning the masses to despair? Do both, some will say. Yet to do both would distort the aim of those who are concerned about self-esteem. Here, then, the aim of providing favorable information that will hopefully change attitudes and behavior collide against the aim of the new social studies which is to develop within students a repertoire of thinking and problem-solving skills.

All these reservations are raised *not to question the value of preparing ethnic materials* but more to clear away the underbrush of rhetoric that has obscured the two goals that I feel can be achieved educationally: to equip students with the necessary skills for clarifying and analyzing what it means and has meant to be black in America; and to expose students to these concepts and generalizations distilled from the black experience in America that are relevant to issues confronting the nation now.

Whether this knowledge and analysis will prop up sagging self-concepts or improve intergroup relations is problematical and must await research evidence. Until then, if pride and self-esteem result, consider them enviable fringe benefits. My chief concern is to set forth goals that can be achieved by the teacher in the classroom.

In short, curriculum materials are limited tools in achieving educational goals. One doesn't sell a hammer to repair a watch nor does one invest materials with promises that cannot be delivered. Materials won't produce attitudinal change. Situations inside and outside school, interaction between students and teachers, and the public climate of opinion —these produce changes. Preparing materials with attitudinal change as a primary aim is energy and talent misplaced.[7]

ASKING THE RIGHT QUESTIONS

The aims of curriculum materials for inner-city youngsters should be skill development and the understanding of

7. What's worse, it is using a bandaid when major surgery is called for. I could, for example, argue for massive desegregation accompanied by extensive teacher-training and re-organization of the school as being the important variables in effecting attitudinal change. There is mounting evidence that a racial and ethnic mix of youngsters in concert with compensatory programs improves achievement and modifies attitudes. Development of curriculum materials to change attitudes would be far down on my list of priorities. But educational shysters continue to peddle materials and curriculum development as a painless and inexpensive short-cut to a pluralistic society.

concepts and generalizations useful in making sense out of what is happening. Having said this, how should a teacher go about preparing these materials, since it must be the teacher who decides ultimately what should be taught and how?

Developing curriculum materials involves four basic questions which apply whenever anyone—teacher, parent, college president, mechanic—sets out to teach anything—facts, principles, skills:

1. What am I going to teach?
2. Why teach it?
3. How should I teach it?
4. Have I taught it?

Questions 1 and 2 deal with the content to be taught and teaching objectives; question 3 focuses upon instruction and will be dealt with in more detail in the next chapter; evaluation is the substance of question 4. Very simple, unoriginal, yet basic to anyone wishing to develop materials and teach.

To answer the four questions intelligently, the teacher must know a number of things. He must know a great deal about who the youngsters are, their hopes and fears, their experiences down to the latest slang word (though he need not speak it), the different homes they come from, what they read and don't read, what they watch on TV, the hit songs, and any other information (without invading privacy) that gives a teacher a rough fix on the interests, concerns, and styles of his students.

The teacher must know the basic concepts, generalizations, and skills of at least one content area, but most important, he should know how to learn—i.e., to internalize the skills of inquiry, problem-solving, and the like. Possessing the generic skills that enable them to teach themselves is critical, because too many teachers are forced to teach out of their field and elementary school teachers are required to be proficient in five or more subject areas. The subject area gives confidence to the teacher; the learning-how-to-learn skills permit intellectual growth. The teacher must know something about learning styles, at least the little that is known at present. A brief word on learning styles.

A handful of social scientists and educators have begun to outline carefully some characteristics of how children learn. Free from the obvious crudities of some of their colleagues, they have paid particular attention to the low-income child. From what I have learned in the classroom and from extensive observations, their very tentative descriptions (note, not prescriptions) have confirmed my primitive efforts to match teaching to learning. Based on what has been identified as characteristics of a learning style, I have fashioned a rough rationale for the development of curriculum materials and teaching strategies for inner-city classrooms.

The low-income youngster first learns by doing and seeing rather than talking and hearing. He has a physical rather than verbal style of learning. In general, such youngsters will score higher on performance tests of intelligence than on the pencil and paper variety. He will often use his fingers when counting or move his lips when reading. These children, Frank Riessman suggets, "work out mental problems best when they can do things physically." Because the school as it is now established rewards speed, word facility, and rapid thinking, the child with a physical learning style (from any income group, I might add) is often labeled a "slow learner." Consider how often poor black, Mexican-American, Appalachian white, and Indian children are placed in mentally retarded classes, basic groups, or whatever the label is.

That students so tagged by schoolmen may not be "slow" is revealed in the surprise of teachers and principals when they discover how supposedly dull students shrewdly connive and manipulate people and rules to cleverly beat the school's regulations. The growing concern about "late bloomers," Job Corps, Upward Bound, New Careers training programs, and the street academies all testify to the sloppy labeling of children by schoolmen.

In most cases, our "slow" students learn differently. They have intellectual strengths and weaknesses that emerge from their basic training in survival. These strengths are often ignored and the weaknesses are too readily exploited by the school to beat down the children.

Another characteristic of learning style lies in the process of thinking. Most of the readers of this book have learned to think in abstractions—nationalism, democracy, militancy—without continually referring to specific examples. We have learned to handle language at a symbolic level. Not so for the low-income child. His style of thinking generally proceeds from the specific to the general. To make sense out of abstractions, ideas must be rooted in experiences of the child and the universal needs of kids. Of course, this is not to say that poor kids cannot conceptualize as well as other children (although short-sighted social scientists and educators have concluded that); it is to say that they differ in *how* they conceptualize.

Such generalizations about a population I characterized as richly diverse suggest a contradiction. The only way I can resolve what appears to be contradictory is to say that the ways poor kids learn is the way all kids learn.

John Holt's book and the work of Jerome Bruner confirmed my hunches and pushed me to re-evaluate how I had learned, to observe my two children more carefully, and to watch and listen closely to what went on in my classes. Putting all this together convinced me that my intuitions were sound: Children learn physically, moving from the specific to the general. As simple as this "discovery" sounds, if implemented on a large scale it would have profound implications for instruction, curriculum, and the organization of the school.

Now what seems to happen is that the verbal style of learning common to middle-class child-rearing is embraced completely by the public school. Remember that Holt's book describes middle- and upper-income kids in private and suburban schools. What he found was that kids learn physically and instruction and curriculum do not capitalize on this; if anything, the school systematically tries to destroy that style. The failures that Holt noted and especially the way kids learned to fail in school is a far more prominent feature in inner-city schools.

Poor children, like their advantaged counterparts, arrive at school ready to learn yet are unequipped to deal with the formalized, highly verbal form of teaching and learning. Styles clash. The school is unmoved since it functions to transform children into respectable middle-class representatives. Students adjust and maladjust in many ways. High drop-out rates, volatile school climates, and low achievement mirror the quality and degree of that adjustment.

A similar confrontation occurs in middle-income schools, but it is muted due to the effects of nursery schools and the convergence of similar values from home and school in creating a competitive, achievement-based climate. In the growing alienation of middle-income adolescents, mounting college drop-out rates, and the analyses of writers such as Holt suggest that the adjustment of well-scrubbed, affluent youngsters is also less than satisfactory.

The physical style of learning applies to all children; it is not peculiar to the poor. The poor, however, suffer from the school's inability to modify instruction, curriculum, and organization; its inability to build upon children's strengths rather than prey on blind spots as it customarily does—i.e., stressing high verbal ability, speed, and the like:[8]

8. Head Start and the Bereiter-Engleman approaches are different strategies in dealing with that early clash in learning styles. Both, in different ways, try to prepare the child for the formal, large-group instruction that characterizes most inner-city classrooms. Bereiter and Engleman (they have since gone their separate ways) developed an approach with low-income pre-school children that diagnosed their difficulties, matched their defects against what has to be learned by a "successful" child in the primary years, and created a structured curriculum and teaching strategy aimed at producing kids with the prerequisite skills and knowledge needed by children in the early elementary years. They asked the four questions I asked earlier, and their answers resulted in the following prescriptions for academic success with inner-city children:

1. Work at different levels of difficulty at different times.
2. Adhere to a rigid, repetitive presentation pattern.
3. Use unison responses whenever possible.
4. Never work with a child individually in a study group for more than 30 seconds.
5. Phrase statements rhythmically.
6. Require children to speak in a loud, clear voice.
7. Do not hurry children or encourage them to talk fast.
8. Clap to accent basic language patterns and conventions.
9. Use questions liberally.
10. Use repetition.

Knowing who the kids are, understanding basic concepts in a field and having the ability to teach one's self, and a knowledge of learning styles are areas that teachers of inner-city youngsters must be conversant with. While this may help to sketch out roughly the content of pre-service teacher education, it only scratches the surface in answering the first of the four questions.

ANSWERING SOME BASIC QUESTIONS

What should be taught to kids depends upon a teacher's knowledge of what his students are interested in and concerned about (and this assumes that the teacher can develop communication with them to find out their interests and concerns), broadened by what the teacher thinks they should

---

11. Be aware of the cues the child is receiving.
12. Use short explanations.
13. Tailor the explanations and rules to what the child knows.
14. Use lots of examples.
15. Prevent incorrect responses whenever possible.
16. Be completely unambiguous in letting the child know when his response is correct and when it is incorrect.
17. Dramatize the use value of learning whenever possible.
18. Encourage thinking behavior.

No words are minced. With "culturally deprived" kids, Bereiter and Engleman promise academic success. Their how-to-do-it book is liberally strewn with specific instructions to the teacher, especially to the prospective teacher, that "there is no mystery surrounding the skills needed to become an effective teacher in an academically oriented preschool." No shilly-shallying around; this no-nonsense approach has shocked the established pre-school movement to its foundations. Based upon Dewey's principles and infused with a strong concern for the total growth of the child, the leaders of the "whole child" movement have attacked the two professors violently. (Carl Bereiter and Siegfried Engleman, *Teaching Disadvantaged Children in the Preschool,* Prentice-Hall, 1966, p. 120.)

be aware of. Deciding on whether the campaigns and strategy of the American Revolutionary War or the anatomy of protest movements get taught must rest upon the teacher's judgment.[9]

Why something should be taught (question 2) gets at the objectives of the content and helps to shape how it is taught (question 3). Assuming, as I have, that skill development is top priority and content is the vehicle, then the real issue becomes why teach one thing and not another. If you are after word attack skills it could be done with a lubrication chart for a Rambler automobile as well as with Shakespeare. Some knowledge has to be taught to get at skills. Deciding what gets taught—to me the single most important decision—forces a teacher to analyze exactly what is and is not essential.

Why study Saratoga, Bunker Hill, and Ticonderoga? Scholars, undoubtedly, can offer substantial reasons for their inclusion in terms of U.S. military history, past and present. But unless a teacher can judge for himself why they should be taught to his students then the reasons are irrelevant. Worse than irrelevant, since scholars' reasons get built into textbooks and unquestioning teachers use them uncritically.

The why, then, means that specific aims have to be stated. Global objectives like "develop good citizenship," "appreciate art," "write clearly," "be creative," "critically think" are pretty useless. You just never know if you have reached those

9. Critics will painstakingly point out that anarchy might develop if twenty teachers go in that many directions. Fragmentation can easily be avoided by team planning between and across grade levels or, more profitably, by curriculum planning at the school level by the faculty.

objectives, and evaluation is critical. The ideal is precision in stating objectives that can be achieved. Although in the arts and humanities the problem is difficult, nevertheless, words like "appreciate" and "understand" are reflections of sloppy thinking and loose, fragmented materials. There is still a wide margin for stating specific objectives that will aid teachers in estimating what, if anything, their students have learned.

Take a unit on protest movements and rebellions as an example. Were I to prepare a unit, I would have to know clearly what concepts and skills I wanted students to acquire and develop. I might, for instance, want students to know:

1. what the word "rebel" means;
2. what the different forms of rebelling are;
3. what surface and underlying causes mean.

And I would want students to be able to:

1. apply their knowledge of different forms of protest and rebelling to a series of newspaper articles;
2. identify surface and underlying causes in a description of a post-football-game riot.

For material, I would use a description of the nature of rebellion, cartoons depicting surface and underlying causes, and a story of a riot. Whatever the material, the more clearly and precisely the objectives are stated, the easier it is to select content that hits what you're after.

What characteristics should material exhibit? I see four components that should be built into curriculum materials. Again, there is little that is original. Experienced teachers will find much that is familiar.

First, materials should be people-centered. Abstract situations should be reduced to human dimensions for students to handle since they, particularly low-income kids, have a vast reservoir of information and experience about how people behave and interpretations of that behavior. Growing up requires them to know adults and one another well if they wish to survive. Such knowledge and interest can be best tapped when materials and teaching situations are structured so that students deal with human behavior and abstract from it concepts and generalizations.

Second, materials should be concrete. Things should be done and wherever possible move from the specific to the abstract. Elementary Science Study materials produced by Educational Services, Inc., (now Education Development Center) in the early 60's directed youngsters to touch, taste, and manipulate items in learning, such as the principles of probability, volume, and so on. Cuisenaire rods follow the same tack in permitting kids to deal concretely with mathematic concepts. At upper levels with older youngsters, increased use of audio-visual devices, especially tape-recorders, still photos, 8-mm film clips, and the like, along with the use of educational games and simulation, provide tangible learning experiences.

Third, conflict should be included in materials wherever possible. By conflict, I mean presenting opposing positions, opinions contrary to those generally held by youngsters, juxtaposing contradictory evidence—all requiring children to make choices. And making choices assumes student evaluation of evidence. Conflict springs from situations where a range of answers are possible, as in the Solomon's baby dilemma or in deciding upon a course of action, say, where values have to be weighed.

Fourth, relevance, a most overworked word. As I use it, relevance refers to tapping students' experiences through examples taken from popular TV programs, current music, dance steps, language, and public issues—kids do discuss intensely and earnestly crime, the draft, Vietnam, and riots. Relevance also refers to learning style—that is, using techniques that play to the strengths of youngsters such as role-playing, manipulating materials, and moving from the specific to the general. Relevance refers to children's feelings. Knowing that hate, anger, love, fear, self-esteem, and power are universal offers excellent opportunities to examine peoples and times far removed from the street corner.

Materials containing these criteria will maximize the chance of making contact with youngsters. In the larger sense, used as tools, curriculum materials try to stimulate the intellectual appetites of children to permit that critical connection between student and teacher to occur, in addition to teaching skills and knowledge. Too often curriculum materials prevent contact and minimize interaction because they are dull, unreadable, or irrelevant; as limited tools they make possible—but in no way guarantee—that a teacher and students can begin to bridge the age, sex, and racial differences that may separate one from the other.

SOME EXAMPLES OF UNITS AND LESSONS

Some example of materials are in order. While I include here printed lessons, audio-visual materials (multi-media to the uninitiated, ranging from still photos, 8-mm film cartridges, unnarrated films, TV programs, records, and tapes) also are curriculum materials, but for obvious reasons cannot be presented here.

Furthermore, space prevents presenting an actual unit which is roughly 5–10 lessons, although a description of one is included.

Given these restraints, the materials presented below contain the necessary components described earlier.

The first lesson is what is known as a "reading." Typically, there is an introduction followed by questions, though not always, and a selection or excerpts from other materials. The selection is often original, sometimes it is adapted or rewritten, and other times it is created especially for a particular purpose. The "readings" format can be used to grade levels 4–12; the ones included below have been used with classes between the eighth and twelfth grades with minor revisions. Remember also that these materials were developed by teacher-interns, who were learning how to teach while in the classroom, and by staff members of the Cardozo Project in Urban Teaching, who were also teaching at least two classes a day.

The first "reading" deals with the concept of due process. The aims, in addition to stimulating interest, were to have the students know what the concept meant and to have them determine whether or not due process was infringed and to judge whether or not the person was guilty, supporting his position with evidence drawn from the selection.

YOU'RE THE JUDGE

The case outlined below (the names have been changed) was recently tried in the United States Court for the District of Columbia. Lawyers, judges, and police alike have admitted that it was a very significant case. Its importance arises not only from the decision in the case itself, but from the effect which that decision has had on other decisions.

Read the evidence presented very closely; unless you thoroughly understand the problems and the facts, you will be unable to make an intelligent decision. I would suggest that you underline those points which seem significant to you and that you read the case twice; the second time around you will have a better idea of what's important.

Consider the following questions:

1. As a judge you must consider not only the evidence (the facts) but also the methods used by the prosecution to obtain that evidence. As you read the case, therefore, underline not only the important facts but also the way in which the facts were collected. Were any of the rights of the accused violated? As a lawyer for the defense, what points would you use to raise doubts as to the legality of the procedures followed by the prosecution?
2. All the evidence below was presented during the course of the trial (although in different form). Do you feel that the police and the U.S. District Attorney have presented enough evidence to prove the guilt of Smith, Jones, and Harris? If so, list the points which seem to justify your position. If not, explain why you think the evidence is incomplete or unsatisfactory.
3. Now, Judge, you've got to make a decision. How will you decide this case? Are the accused "not guilty," "guilty," or what? As a judge you *must* justify your decision because your finding will be referred to by other judges and lawyers in other cases of this type.

The Court will come to order. The District Court of the District of Columbia will hear the case brought by the *United States vs. John Jones and James Smith.*

John Jones and James Smith were arrested on Friday, March 9, 1962, at 9:45 P.M., on suspicion of having committed a purse-snatching. They were arrested because they fit the description of the purse-snatchers and because they had no satisfactory explanation for being in the area in which the robbery was committed. They were brought to police headquarters, Precinct #13, for a lineup. The 17-year-old Jones was thereupon released to his parents. Smith, however, was kept in jail overnight, although he was not charged with a crime nor suspected of having committed one. The purse-snatching is not connected with the case which we are examining here.)

The next morning at 8:15 A.M. (Saturday, March 10), Smith was placed in a line-up at #1 Precinct. This line-up included people picked up from all over the city for a variety of offenses. In the audience were police officers from all over the city who had come to see the line-up in hope of picking up men they had been looking for. Among the officers was officer Preston of the Homicide Squad, for Preston had heard that Smith had been picked up on the purse-snatching at a point very close to the spot where Miska Merson had been murdered the week before.

Officer Preston noticed that Smith was wearing a jacket which appeared to have blood stains on it. This fact impressed him enough to cause him to take Smith to the offices of the Homicide Squad for questioning.

There officer Preston questioned him about his whereabouts of the night before and also asked him where he had been on the night of the Merson murder. On the night of the murder, Smith claimed, he had entered a theatre about 7:30 P.M., although he could remember neither the name of the picture nor the name of the theatre. Preston noticed the fact that Smith had been specific only about the time (7:30 P.M.) which was almost the moment when Merson had died. Preston asked Smith if Jones had accompanied him to the theatre; Smith replied that Jones had not been with him.

At 10:05 A.M. of the same morning, Smith consented to have his finger and palm prints taken. Several days later it was discovered that these prints were the same as those found on an anonymous letter containing some of Merson's personal effects. This letter had been sent to the police.

At 10:30 A.M. officer Preston asked officer Eccles to go to Jones' home. Officer Eccles was instructed to question Jones concerning his whereabouts on the night of the murder. Preston hoped that he would be able to connect Jones with Smith and with the slaying of Merson.

At about 11:20 A.M. Smith consented to taking a lie-detector test; the test ran from about 11:30 A.M. to 2:00 P.M. During the trial officer Preston testified that by the time the test had been concluded he had become convinced that Smith had lied, that Smith was "in fact, involved with the homicide."

Meanwhile officer Eccles had gone to the home of Jones in the company of another officer. Officer Eccles was greeted by Jones' mother; he told her that the police wanted to find out if Jones had been with Smith. He also told her that he wanted to take Jones down to police headquarters. Jones' mother consented to this and she called Jones out of bed.

When Jones came down stairs, officer Eccles told him that he wanted Jones to come down town to "try and clear Smith." Jones agreed. Officer Eccles testified during the trial that he would not have arrested the boy if Jones had refused to come.

About half an hour after Eccles and Jones arrived at police headquarters, Eccles noticed that Jones was wearing a round, gold watch with a sweep second hand. Eccles did not advise Jones of his right to refuse to answer questions nor of his right to an attorney. Instead, he immediately questioned Jones about the watch. Jones claimed that he had gotten it from his mother.

Officer Eccles immediately went to the outer office where Jones' mother was waiting and asked her about the watch. She denied having given the watch to the boy. Eccles then returned to Jones and confronted him with his mother's denial. At that point Jones changed his tune and claimed that he had gotten the watch from another boy. He claimed that when he received the watch from the boy he had exchanged the band for the gold band. Officer Eccles knew that Merson's watch had had a gold band. At that point, therefore, he arrested Jones for the murder of Miska Merson.

When officer Preston had completed Smith's lie-detector test, officer Eccles took in Jones. Jones' mother was not asked for her permission before the test was given. Jones' test began at 2 P.M. when Smith's test ended, and lasted until about 6 P.M. Finally, after the test was completed, Jones admitted that he knew about the murder of Merson, but he claimed that Smith had done it, and that Smith had told him about it.

A few minutes after 6 P.M., officer Preston brought Smith and Jones face-to-face. Smith still maintained that he had nothing to do with the murder, and Jones then denied that Smith had had anything to do with the murder. Smith was then taken to a cell block and Jones was taken away to another office for further questioning. At this point Jones changed his mind again, in fact he broke down completely and admitted his involvement in the crime. In addition, Jones told the officers that he would show them the escape route which he and Smith had used.

At 6:45 P.M. officer Preston and another policeman took Jones to the scene of the crime. Jones showed him the spot where he and Smith had divided the spoils of the robbery and the place where they had discarded some of the victim's belongings. Then Jones and the officers returned to police headquarters, where Jones was given his first food of the day; a sandwich. At headquarters Jones signed a written statement in which he admitted taking the wallet from the victim, that Smith had taken the victim's watch, and that Smith had hit Merson twice with a club, causing his death.

Immediately after the statement was taken, a lawyer appeared for the first time, about 8 or 8:15 P.M. The attorney had been hired by Jones' mother, who asked him to find out why her son was being held by the police. For this she paid him $20. The lawyer entered the office in which Jones was being held. Officer Preston heard the attorney tell Jones that "he should tell the truth, be entirely truthful and clear it up." Officer Preston did not hear the attorney tell Jones that he had the right to remain silent if he wished.

Jones was then turned over to the Juvenile Squad, placed

in the Receiving Home and charged with homicide.

Between 6 P.M. and midnight of that same Saturday, police officers discussed the case with an Assistant United States District Attorney to determine whether or not Smith should be brought before the District Commissioner for arraignment. The District Attorney told the officers that there was not yet enough evidence to bring the case before the Commissioners. He further advised them that Smith, who had been held for 24 hours already, should be held in custody for a reasonable length of time for further questioning.

On Sunday morning, March 11th, beginning at approximately 10:30 A.M., Smith was questioned by officer Preston again. This time, Smith broke down, and he admitted his part in the homicide, and said that there was a third person (later to be named Harris) also involved. Thus the police gained their first knowledge of Harris' participation in the crime, at 11:30 on Sunday morning.

In the course of his oral confession, Smith admitted that it was he who had struck Merson with the limb in order to take his valuables. Merson was selected apparently because he happened to find a parking place in the street in which the men were waiting.

At some point during the confession, Smith requested that Jones be brought in to listen to the confession. The officers agreed, and about noon, Jones was brought from the Receiving Home to the office in which Smith was being questioned. No attorney was present. At that time, Jones and Smith called the third person "Red." From the description which Smith and Jones provided, the police were able to identify Harris.

Smith then accompanied the officers to the scene of the crime. There Smith showed them the escape route which Jones previously showed them, and he also located a small purse which he (Smith) had discarded on the night of the murder. Prior to this the police had known nothing about the purse.

They returned to the office of the Homicide Squad about 2:15 P.M. There Smith dictated a written statement. At about 4 P.M. the victim's brother came to the office; Smith admitted the crime to the brother and apologized to him. Jones also admitted the crime to the brother. Smith was then returned to the cell block; Jones and Harris, who had been arrested that morning and charged with homicide, were returned to the Receiving Home.

On Monday, March 12, at 10:00 A.M., Smith was taken before the District Commissioner. At that time he was advised to remain silent and of his right to consult a lawyer. No attorney was present at the office of the Commissioner at the time, however.

By this time Smith had been in custody over 60 hours since the time he was arrested on suspicion of purse-snatching on Friday night. During all of this time, Smith was never advised that he was entitled to an attorney. Later, officer Preston testified that both before the lie-detector test on Saturday and before the interrogation on Sunday Smith was advised that he did not have to make a statement.

On Wednesday, March 14th, a coroner's inquest [inquiry] was held. Smith was present, and was represented by an attorney, employed by the legal aid agency (which furnishes lawyers to those people who lack the money to pay for them), who advised Smith to make no statement. Harris testified as a witness and was represented by an attorney. Jones apparently had no attorney of his own.

On Thursday, March 15th, officer Preston brought Smith's girlfriend to see him; Smith had requested that he be allowed to see her on the preceding Sunday. They arrived about 11:15 A.M. Shortly after noon, Smith came in.

The officer testified that the usual practice was for the prisoner and his relative to talk over a speaker system, while they were separated by a glass panel. On this occasion, however, Smith, the girlfriend, and officer Preston sat together at a table in the jail. The officer later admitted that he was aware that he might get information by listening in on the conversation.

Preston overheard the entire conversation, which included a statement by Smith that he had killed Merson, although he had intended only to rob him. Smith then turned to officer Preston and asked him if he thought that he (Smith) should get a lawyer. The officer later testified that he told Smith "that I thought he needed the best lawyer that he could get." Smith gave his girlfriend a telephone number of a person who, Smith thought, might help him get a lawyer. Officer Preston *then* told Smith that he might testify in court to anything which Smith might say, but Smith continued to talk anyway. At 12:40 P.M., officer Preston and the girlfriend left the jail.

On Friday, March 23rd, the Juvenile Court decided that Jones should be tried as an adult. He was brought to police headquarters and jailed.

Another example of a reading is a high school lesson on a black politician during Reconstruction. Try to answer the questions and complete the exercise to see if any skill operations are being used.

FRANCIS L. CARDOZO: POLITICIAN

To the southern slaveholder, the world had turned upside down. An ex-slave, Blanche K. Bruce was now sitting in the United States Senate seat of Jefferson Davis of Mississippi. A Negro Senator from Mississippi. Imagine! Pinckney Benton Pinchback sat—only for a short time—in the Louisiana's governor mansion. Throughout the South, whites rubbed their eyes in disbelief; it looked as if the bottom social class had become the top social class. Black militia, black legislators, black judges. It was unheard of before and since. Negroes and whites ran the University of South Carolina, where one black professor—Richard T. Greener—taught logic and philosophy to integrated classes. It was truly the beginning of a new day for the South. For a brief moment in history, the United States tried to make the Declaration of Independence come alive; tried to make democracy more than a word. But it was brief—only a little more than a decade. And then it was gone from the South.

Yet to look at most textbooks, one seldom finds any mention of these black individuals who made a name for themselves. What we find, unfortunately, are the weaknesses, the failings of this experiment. Corruption, graft, scandals that marked Reconstruction state governments are given great emphasis to "prove" that black and white could not govern well. Even though no state government was dominated by Negroes, the corruption is cited as evidence of *incompetence.* Overlooked is the tremendous amounts of money stolen by political bosses in New York or the scandals that rocked Congress in these years.

In effect, the negative side of Reconstruction—the increase in crime, use of political influence, etc.—have been emphasized to the neglect of the solid achievements worked out by whites and Negroes in many areas of the South. Carpetbaggers and scalawags—northerners and southerners who took advantage of unsettled conditions and made money—have received far more attention and have overshadowed the successes of Radical Reconstruction.

As a result of the unbalanced treatment of these years in most textbooks, a large number of *myths* have grown up. One story is that black politicians of these southern states were illiterate, ignorant fieldhands fresh off the cotton patch. Many elected officials were illiterate and unfamiliar with the rules of politics.

But it is well to remember that formal education was not crucial to success. Lincoln never had an education beyond the lower grades; Andrew Johnson didn't learn how to read until he was an adult. What is far more important is initiative, drive, intelligence, foresight, and ability to speak. Some Negro leaders of this period possessed these traits; some did not. Perhaps the best way of deciding about the role of the black politician during Reconstruction is to realize that SOME Negroes, like whites, stole; that SOME Negroes, like whites, were uneducated and ignorant, that SOME Negroes, like whites, joined with those northerners and southerners out to make a fast buck. These things did occur. But to generalize the SOME into ALL goes beyond the facts.

Let us examine the career of one particular black man of the period who was not nationally known yet achieved a position of power in one Reconstructed state. Such an examination may give us an insight into the role played by Negro politicians. Let's look at Francis L. Cardozo of South Carolina.

As you read, consider the following questions: In the first selection:

1. What obstacles did Cardozo have to overcome?
2. What opportunities did he take advantage of?

LIFE AND TIMES OF FRANCIS L. CARDOZO

Charleston, South Carolina in 1837 was a southern city with definite ideas about how Negroes should behave and where they belonged. Slavery was considered the natural state for all Negroes and for the free colored community of Charleston, life was—at best—*precarious.* The threat of returning to slavery hung heavy over the heads of all free Negroes. Discrimination and prejudice forced a second-class status upon them. What freedom they had depended upon the good-will of certain upper-class whites. It was into this community that Francis L. Cardozo, son of a Jewish economist and a mulatto woman, was born.

Two important events marked his childhood. He had the opportunity to go to school at the age of five and at the age of twelve he was apprenticed to a carpenter for four years. While school equipped him with skills many of his racial brothers lacked, it also generated a desire to continue his education. The skilled trade enabled him to set aside money to continue his education. By the time he was twenty-one, he had saved $1000 and with this money he sailed for Scotland to get a college education. Don't think it strange for a free Negro to leave the country to secure an education, for only one or two colleges in the country even admitted black students at this time.

For four years, Cardozo studied in Scotland and England. The total cost was $4000. Where did he get the money? A quarter of that he had saved from carpentering. Another $1000 he earned working at the trade during the summers and vacations. In competition among graduates of a number of English colleges, he won a $1000 scholarship. The remainder came from a fifth prize in Latin and a seventh prize in Greek won in competition with other students.

Cardozo returned to the United States a year before the Civil War ended and became pastor of a Congregational Church in New Haven, Connecticut. Though the church was important to Cardozo, he firmly believed that education and politics offered greater opportunities for the betterment of the race. The following year, at the age of 28, he returned to Charleston to become principal of a school for Negroes. It was here that he became active in the political reconstruction of South Carolina.

In January, 1868 a Convention met to draw up a new Constitution as directed by Congress. Cardozo was elected as a delegate. As a delegate he was opposed to needless *expenditure* on the part of other delegates. He also believed that the plantation system should be destroyed and land be made available to whites and Negroes at low prices. As a result of his efforts as delegate, he became well known. In August of 1868, he was elected Secretary of State of South Carolina. While holding this position he never lost his deep interest in education. In fact, Howard University offered him a professorship in Latin. He did teach at Howard for a short time and then returned to South Carolina to accept the office of Treasurer. During his term, he handled upwards of $15,000,000. Scandals, however, involving theft of public funds cast a shadow over Cardozo. He was accused of improper handling of public funds, and was investigated by the South Carolina legislature. Accountants checked his books minutely and could not uncover any instances of wrong-doing. As a result, he was absolved of all charges. His reputation was cleared. Unfortunately, this was the period of growing white resentment and illegal activity against governments supported by "Radical" Republicans. Little opportunity or future existed for Negro statesmen.

In 1877, Cardozo was appointed to a clerkship in the U.S. Post Office in Washington, D.C. Cardozo accepted the appointment, especially since Wade Hampton, former slaveholder, was elected Governor of South Carolina and Reconstruction was over for that state. Six years later, Cardozo was appointed principal of the colored high school, now Dunbar High School. He remained there until his death in 1903.

EXERCISE

For each of the following, mark Probably True (PT) for a statement that is supported by evidence in the selection; Probably False (PF) for a statement that goes against the evidence in the selection; Needs Evaluation (NE) for a statement that is not related to any evidence in the selection. For each answer supply the statement that supports your answer.

______ a. Cardozo was born a slave ______________

______ b. Cardozo worked hard to take advantage of the opportunities that came his way ______________

____

______ c. He had above average intelligence ______________

______ d. Cardozo stole money from the government ______

______ e. Minister, public official, teacher, post office clerk and principal, Cardozo had many job experiences

____

This brief outline of Cardozo's life offers little insight into what the man was like. Howard Fast, author of *Freedom Road,* casts Cardozo as a major character in his novel of Reconstruction days in South Carolina. His view of Cardozo, though fictional, may give us a few insights into what the man was like. The first excerpt describes the meeting of some of the Negro delegates to the Constitutional Convention. Most of the delegates meeting in Cardozo's house were educated, had been free for many years, and entertained doubts about the future of the Negro in South Carolina. One delegate, Gideon Jackson, had just been freed from slavery. Illiterate, but intelligent, Jackson seemed out of place among the cultured, well-dressed Negroes. His manners were crude, his speech was rough, yet Gideon had ambition, drive, and a great deal of hope. One delegate asked him what his opinion of the Constitution being written was. "What will you want in a Constitution you have a part in making?"

> Gideon looked at them, the heavy-set Nash, the slim, almost courtly Cardozo, Wright, round and suave, like a well-fed house servant. And the room they sat in, a room that to Gideon seemed elegant almost beyond belief, upholstered chairs, a stuffed squirrel, even a rug on the floor, and three crayon pictures on the walls. How does a black man come by all this? Where did he fit into it? And the other delegates who had plodded across the state in their shapeless cotton-field boots?
>
> Gideon nodded. . . . "I guess you want an answer. Talk about a man who can't read, can't write, just an old nigger come walking out of the cotton fields, that's me. What I want from Constitution? Maybe it ain't what you folks want —want learning, want it for all, black and white. Want a freedom that's sure as an iron fencepost. Want no man should push me off the street. Want a little farm where a

nigger can put in a crop and take out a crop all his days. That's what I want."

Then there was a silence, and Gideon felt embarrassed, provocative and high and mighty without reason, a man who said a lot, none of it making sense. A little later, the others made their goodbyes, but when Gideon rose to go, Cardozo plucked at his sleeve and begged him to wait a moment. And when the others had left, said to Gideon:

"Have some tea, please, and we can talk. It wasn't so clever of me, bringing you into this, was it?"

"That's all right," Gideon nodded, wanting to go, but too unsure of himself to know how to go about his leave-taking. Cardozo's wife came in then, a small, pretty brown woman. Gideon loomed over her like a giant.

Cardozo said, "Won't you stay? There's a lot for us to talk about." Gideon nodded.

"Then look at it this way," Cardozo said. "Here were a few of us who have been free Negroes, maybe not as close to our people as we should have been. Just a few of us, against the four million slaves. But the books were opened to us, and we learned a little; but believe me, in a way we were more slaves than you. Now here comes a situation so strange, so open in its implications, that the world cannot fully realize it. The Union government, backed with a military machine it built during the war, says to the people of the South, white and black, build a new life. From the beginning. A new Constitution, new laws, a new society. The white planters rebel against this, but they are defeated. Yet they stay away from the voting, and as a result here in this state black men, slaves only yesterday, choose their own people and send them to the Convention. Do you know, Gideon, that we, the blacks, are in the majority, that over fifty of these are former slaves? This is the year eighteen-sixty-eight; how long have we been out of bondage? The Children of Israel wandered in the wilderness for forty years."

After a moment, Gideon murmured, "I don't quote Scripture when I'm afraid. I'm a God-fearing man, but when the fright was strongest inside of me, I took a gun in my hands and fought for my freedom."

"And what will these field-hands do in the courts of law?"

"What they do? They ain't no black savages, like newspapers say. They got a wife and child and love in their hearts. They say what is good for me, for woman, for the child, and they vote that in. They got a hunger for learning, and they vote for that. They know about slavery, and they vote for freedom. They ain't going to be uppity; you lead them by the hand, and by God, they come. But you don't take no lash to their back no more. They know how it taste to be a free man."

Thoughtfully, Cardozo said, "That'll take courage from me, Gideon."

"Took courage from me to come to this Convention."

"I suppose so. Tell me something about yourself, Gideon."

The telling came slow and stumblingly from Gideon; it was nightfall when he had finished. He felt dry and used up. But before he left, Cardozo gave him two books, one *Geldon's Basic Speller* and the other *Usage of the English Language. . . .* They were the first real books Gideon ever had; he held them gently in his big hands, as if they were made of eggshell. Plucking a name from his memory, he asked;

"You got the Shakespeare book?"

For a moment, Cardozo hesitated; then, without smiling he went to his little shelf of books, took *Othello* and handed it to Gideon.

"Thank you," Gideon said.

And Cardozo nodded, and after Gideon had left, said to his wife, "If I had laughed—If I had! God help me, I almost laughed! What animals we are!"

Gideon asked Carter [the family with whom Gideon was

staying] to tell him something about Cardozo. . . . Carter was impressed by the fact that Gideon had been to Cardozo's home. . . .

"He's part Jew," Carter said. "That's how he come by his name. He's a proud nigger."

Gideon, who had never seen a Jew before, said, "Looks the same like any black man."

"But uppity," Carter said.

Cardozo lay awake [that night] thinking about Gideon. Like a gap in his life, like a gap in human history, in the whole aching, crawling stream of human life was that space left on his shelf after he had removed the three books. How did he come to Gideon Jackson? Who was this huge, slow-moving, slow-spoken, black man who had come out of the Carolina back country, out of slavery, out of darkness, and why did he make Cardozo feel so small? What was the measure of a man? He, Cardozo, had been born free; in his memories there was an education at the University of Glasgow (Scotland); there were garden parties outside of London. There was a great meeting where he had addressed three thousand Englishmen, and had been accorded honor and respect. He had crossed oceans and been in the homes of the great.

He had been a minister in New Haven, and Abolitionists had met in his house and spun their plots. There was in his veins white blood and black, Negro and Indian, Jew and *Gentile* spun together. Even the white men of Charleston accorded him respect. He, Cardozo, was closer to a [southern aristocrat] than Gideon Jackson was to him.

Yet he recognized in Gideon Jackson the salvation, if there was to be any in this dark confusion; the huge illiterate black man was looking at sunshine which Cardozo did not see. Cardozo, who could not sleep because his fears were so many, his ambitions so hopeless, lay awake and envied a free slave.[10]

10. Copyright: Howard Fast, 1944.

QUESTIONS

1. What similarities were there between Cardozo and Gideon Jackson?
2. What differences were there between the two?
3. Why does Cardozo envy the illiterate, poor Jackson?

A UNIT

Perhaps a better insight into curriculum materials might be a description of a unit rather than one lesson. Units contain the student material, verbal and non-verbal, generally to be used over a period of a week or two, no longer. Teachers' manuals accompany the student units to clarify, explain, and suggest how each lesson in the unit might be used.

Tight, short units were developed purposely to meet the learning style of youngsters in terms of structuring of material—i.e., each unit had a definite beginning, middle, and end with exercises interlaced throughout to consolidate what has been learned.

Also, we felt that in short units integrated knowledge would be achieved in the student's mind rather than solely in the teacher's mind.

Jay Mundstuk, a former intern and later a colleague of mine while I was at Cardozo, described a unit that he, another teacher—Isaac Jamison—and I developed over one summer. Space does not permit its inclusion but Mundstuk's description captures the answers to the initial four questions I emphasized earlier and includes the necessary components for materials. The unit was on the assassination of President John F. Kennedy.

Our first concern was to teach a series of reasoning skills which would be needed in all courses as well as outside the classroom. The content was admittedly secondary; in choosing it, we were searching for a subject on which material readily was available, which was "open" enough to give students an opportunity to apply critical intelligence and genuinely come to their own conclusions. [In so many cases, students are supposed to develop their own conclusions, but the material is such that it precludes all but the conclusion preordained by the teacher or curriculum writer. While this has its value it tends to take the bite out of the process of inquiry.] Finally, we wanted a subject that would take hold of our students—that would capture their imagination and concern and engage their minds in trying to figure out some answers.

The Kennedy assassination provided an almost ideal answer. Material about the assassination is abundant; both primary sources in the form of testimony before the Warren Commission and the flood of attacks and defenses that have been heaped upon the conclusions of the commission. Further, the memory of President Kennedy is very dear to many of our students. We were given a hint of the extent of their affection for Kennedy when at the beginning of the year, we asked students to evaluate Johnson as a President. A majority of the students volunteered that Johnson couldn't hold a candle to Kennedy, whom they named as the best President we have ever had. The mystery of Lee Harvey Oswald and his role in the assassination had piqued our students' curiosity. And the answer to the question, "Who killed Kennedy?" now more than ever, is an open one with no final answer.

The material was organized into a series of lessons which, first, raised the question of how we know who the assassin of President Kennedy was [to have students question their half-articulated beliefs], then presented them with available evidence upon which conclusions have been drawn. As the students sorted through the evidence, they had to learn to use a series of skills:

1. How to make and verify hypotheses.
2. How to evaluate the reliability of sources of evidence.
3. How to weigh evidence and to use it in support of a reasoned conclusion.
4. How to distinguish between facts [verifiable statements] and opinions.
5. How to distinguish between relevant and irrevelant information in reaching conclusions.
6. How to draw inferences from a set of facts.

In addition, students had to read carefully and to write reasonably well-argued essays, using evidence to support their views.

Let it be clear; it was not our purpose to "prove" Oswald innocent or guilty. The unit asks students to read the available sources, examine and reach conclusions that will stand close scrutiny. We are more concerned with the process of drawing conclusions—a process embodying the skills we outlined above—than the conclusion itself.

What Is in the Unit?

To begin this process, our first lesson seeks to recall the events of that day in Dallas through pictures, headlines, and personal accounts of how the news affected people, getting students to relate their feelings about the central question of the unit: How do we know Oswald is the assassin? As an assignment, students will write an essay on this question.

In the second lesson, two journalistic accounts detail the "facts" of the assassination and the evidence against Oswald. Here the student establishes a sequence of events, begins to build a case against Oswald and simultaneously sees that the accounts from *Newsweek* and *Time* are imperfect sources of evidence since they both contain a number of discrepancies.

The next two lessons aim at building a lawyer's case for or against Oswald over and above the information students have obtained up to this point. Eyewitness accounts, rebuttals of their testimony and irrelevant material are included to force students to interpret evidence. Since the rebuttal of some of the eyewitness testimony can be very persuasive some students may even begin to question their own prejudices, i.e., conclusions based upon fragmentary, biased evidence.

To highlight the case against Oswald we can take one of the "facts" against him (Oswald was a good enough shot to have killed the President, a moving target, with three quick shots, at a distance of over two hundred yards) and examine it very closely in the next lesson. Students will see how conflicting statements make it very difficult to draw an accurate conclusion that satisfies the available evidence.

At this point, the case against Oswald contains strong circumstantial evidence against him yet certain facts had been introduced that carried enough weight to raise questions about Oswald's guilt. Thus, the big question of the unit concerning whether Oswald can be definitely pinpointed as the assassin should remain open to those members of the class evaluating the evidence impartially.

In the next lesson, we shift to an investigation of Oswald himself. If previous lessons were concerned with establishing his presence at the scene of the murder and his ability as a marksman, then it is time to turn to motive. Did he have a reason to kill the President? The reading drawn from his diary and comments from people who have known him, suggest that it is virtually impossible to ascertain a motive. Students discover this by proposing hypotheses about the motive and exposing them to class scrutiny.

With all of this information presented to the student, we move to a lesson that will force the student to organize this material into categories. This lesson is structured as a game in which groups of students compete to see who can most accurately categorize a series of statements concerning the assassination and defend their choices satisfactorily.

This game is followed by a day of review that permits

> each of the above groups the opportunity to defend or prosecute Oswald, making use of what has been learned up to this point.
>
> The last day of the unit tests the students on their knowledge and the skills they have developed. The last part of the test asks the student to write an essay on the same question they wrote on the first lesson of the unit. While not the most sophisticated measuring device, this essay should reflect the growth, if any, in expression and skill development as contrasted with the first essay.

Evaluative instruments are still primitive, especially those devised by classroom teachers like ourselves. We relied upon teachers' and students' responses and grade distribution of the unit test compared to previous performance. It is all soft data, vulnerable to criticism, but we offer it as evidence that it is both important and imperative that classroom teachers make a stab at assessing their own and student' performance on materials. Mundstuk describes what we did.

> We taught the unit to a total of 15 classes at Cardozo during the first three weeks of the semester [1966]. Eight of the classes were in U.S. History, four were 9th grade Civics classes and two in Modern European History, an honors track class, and 12th grade government. Since the unit concentrates on those skills which are essential to the study of all social sciences, we felt justified in teaching it to the wide range of classes.
>
> With the exception of the Modern European History classes, all of our students were in the General Track. These are usually students who are uncommitted to college or vocational choices, ranging in reading skill from a minority at grade level to two to four years below grade level, and even lower. It is these non-college bound students who have been largely ignored by recent curriculum development experimentation and for whom the usual social studies curriculum

has little relevance. We were particularly eager to develop material which would engage this group and at the same time help them develop and improve their skills. . . .

Interest was very high in the beginning, and although it tapered off for some students during the three weeks it took to teach the unit, most students were with us throughout the unit. Many students did extra reading on the assassination and found themselves discussing the material with their parents and friends. Students are still bringing up the subject from time to time, sometimes bringing in newspaper clippings as the running debate over the Warren Report continues. Some students became obsessed with the question: one intern reported that one of his students confessed that he lay awake at night trying to figure out whether Oswald was guilty or innocent.

Incidentally, this involvement on the part of some students led to frustration, when, toward the end, many of them realized that in the final analysis, the question could not have a solid answer.

The most striking aspect of the classroom sessions during those three weeks was the quality of student exchanges. Students engaged in lusty debate in the classroom, thus breaking the usual pattern of teacher dominated discussion. Although some students made use of this opportunity to pursue a form of one-up-manship—"I can defend Oswald better than you can"—most of them quickly became involved in a matching of wits that demanded thought and command of the subject matter. Many of us found students asking for additional information to use as ammunition and to clear up murky points. And this is what we were trying to get.

Some Problems

One of our purposes in teaching the unit was to raise doubts in the kids' minds about the reliability of information. We were asking them to question the sources of their knowledge and to develop a certain skepticism toward "facts" which were unverified. There was no problem in doing this, but we may have overshot the mark in some cases. In fact, there were far fewer believers in the conclusions of the Warren Commission than we had anticipated. Some were ready to support a conspiraacy theory with Lyndon Johnson at its heart. But once students saw how ambiguous supposedly conclusive evidence may be upon close scrutiny, and how difficult it was to establish facts in this case, many swung to the extreme of believing nothing. By the end of the unit, we had a group of skeptics on our hands who were ready to throw out most of our historical knowledge on the grounds of insufficient evidence. Perhaps, were we to teach the unit again, we might place more emphasis upon what *can* be reasonably accepted from the evidence—for instance, that Oswald was definitely involved.

Did We Teach Them Anything?

The high interest and participation was mirrored in the test results. The objective part of the unit test asked students to make use of the skills we had tried to teach, rather than recall factual information [although some recall was necessary for sections of the test]. The students did well. In most cases, we found a solid normal distribution of grades, skewed somewhat to the higher side. In some classes, almost all students scored A or B. The test also included an essay which asked students to defend or prosecute Oswald; although the results of this essay ranged widely, we found considerable improvement in the quality of the work over the first essay. The major difference was that students were using specific evidence they had obtained from the unit to support their point of view—a significant change from reliance upon hearsay or vague feelings which was so prevalent in the first attempt. . . .

With these students, many of whom are in the General Track, the "typical" normal distribution of grades is highly atypical, and the quality of written work is often poor. Further, lively exchanges in the classroom between students dealing knowledgeably with the subject under discussion do not often occur—at least, when the more traditional approaches are used. That these students did engage in such discussion and did produce solid work is an indication, we think, of success of the material in involving the students and engaging their concern and of the potential that does exist among these students when it is tapped.

What the Students Said

But we didn't want to leave the evaluation to only impressions. After completing the unit, we went to the kids to find out how they felt. We asked them, anonymously, to grade the unit, evaluate each lesson and comment on some of their reactions to the unit.

Summary

—Students enjoyed studying the unit. Sixty per cent graded it "A," and another 36.3% gave it a "B" rating. There were no D's or F's.

—The most popular lesson was the first—*Time* and *Newsweek* accounts of the day of the assassination. The freshness of the material and the drama of the accounts probably accounts for its slight lead in popularity. The least favored was, interestingly the game, "How Good a Lawyer Are You," in which all students were asked to classify facts and opinions as tending to convict or acquit Oswald. A majority of the students, however, found all the lessons interesting.

—Almost all students felt the unit should be taught to other classes.

—Students disagreed on the conclusion they reached at the end of the unit. Some felt Oswald's guilt had been confirmed; others finished the study confused about his guilt.

—A small but noticeable proportion of students objected to the argument that took place in class and some others said they didn't like the difficulty they had in coming to a conclusion.

—Many students felt that it was important for Americans

to know about the assassination. This was one of the most important reasons for having other classes study the unit.

—A number of students said the unit helped them to learn to think better.

—A large minority—36.1%—felt their understanding had not changed. Most of them meant that they began thinking Oswald was guilty and ended believing the same thing.

Figures and Student Comments

1. Overall evaluation of the unit:

A	B	C	D	F
145	*90*	*14*	*0*	*9*
60.0%	*36.3%*	*3.7%*		

2. Rating of individual lessons:

LESSONS		INTERESTING	AVERAGE	DULL
The Assassination	No.	*193*	*42*	*3*
	%	*81.7%*	*17.6%*	*1.3%*
What Does the Evidence Say?	No.	*176*	*50*	*12*
	%	*74.0*	*20.8*	*5.2*
Oswald, The Marksman	No.	*141*	*80*	*10*
	%	*61.0*	*34.7*	*4.3*
Was There a Motive?	No.	*175*	*51*	*17*
	%	*72.0*	*21.0*	*7.0*

How Good a Lawyer Are You?	No.	*137*	*85*	*14*
	%	*58.1*	*36.0*	*5.9*

3. Should this unit be taught to other social studies classes?

YES	NO
238	*9*
96.3%	*3.7%*

In this, students were almost unanimous. Students pointed to the importance of the subject for Americans and to the unit's stimulus to thinking as their reasons. Some representative comments:

". . . it is so important to Americans that it should be taught."

". . . it will stimulate their minds."

"It will help other students . . . to think like adults instead of taking what people say."

"Because it is very interesting. . . ."

"It is worth knowing the truth. . . ."

". . . it helps your understanding and [makes you] *think*."

"[No] because this [is] too dull and boring and too much reading and homework."

4. Has your understanding changed?

YES	NO
157	*85*
64.9%	*36.1%*

This question touched off some interesting comment. Some students felt the unit confirmed Oswald's guilt; others don't know what to believe. And a good many students made some thoughtful comments about what they learned from the unit quite apart from the question of Oswald's guilt. Here is what they said:

"I have changed because I thought Oswald was the assassin, but this story gives you a chance to look on both sides."

"I think I can understand Oswald and why he did most of the things he did."

"My understanding has matured."

"A person is innocent until proven guilty."

"I still think Oswald is guilty but now I have to recognize the fact that he could be innocent, and open to all points of view."

"I am still not positive but the possibilities are broadened so I can draw a much better conclusion *if I ever do!*"

"I have now learned to look at both sides and not just conclude from one."

"At first I was sure Oswald but now I'm unbalanced."

"After having been exposed to both sides of the story and to all evidence, I think Oswald was framed."

". . . I know that all I read are not facts. . . ."

". . . I think they should reopen the case. . . ."

"This assignment gave me a new way to look at things and not be one-sided about the possible truths."

Admittedly, our evaluation has a Gee Whiz ring to it. I confess that there is much amateurism to it, yet isn't the classroom teacher the person who must begin assessing his performance by the students' reactions and their achievement? Asking the first three questions without the fourth cuts off the teacher and student from ever evaluating what happened in the class. Maybe it is primitive, still a beginning has to be made.

OBSTACLES FACING TEACHERS

Stressing the necessity of every teacher asking the four questions is one thing; it is another thing to have them do it in view of the obstacles that schools place before teachers. Teachers have good cause to shy away from preparing curriculum materials for their classes. Count the reasons.

- No time for research.
- No space and materials to prepare lessons and units.
- Supervisors often want teachers to follow the course of study.
- City-wide tests.
- By diverging from prescribed materials, students won't be prepared for college.

Like all obstacles, they can be perceived as barriers to overcome or excuses to do nothing.

Lack of time and assistance are valid reasons. Fear of constraint from supervisors is largely myth in inner-city schools since they don't have line authority over teachers and they aren't around enough. Even the most ambitious, most aggressive supervisor or department head would not be able to visit a particular teacher's class more than once a month and that would be a generous estimate. Even were that the case, sharp teachers ingeniously prepare for such visits—the word of a supervisor's arrival spreads quickly—by prepping kids or trotting out conventional lessons.

If anything, a strange eerie freedom pervades most inner-city classrooms. Once the door closes, teachers do pretty much what they want to do and only the student grapevine reveals peep-hole glances at what transpires in a class. In most cases, teachers follow the text or guidelines laid down; some chuck these aside and use what they can salvage in an attempt to teach creatively; still others could teach a racing sheet to students and no one would know the difference. Recent student protests across the nation, of course, opened the classroom door somewhat and broke the conspiracy of silence over what does happen in the classroom.

If freedom is a false issue, so are college boards and city- or state-wide tests. Teaching academic and problem-solving skills over the school year helps prepare youngsters for the tests, because many of these tests have become more skill-based than tests of information. If the tests are still information-based or the teacher fears that his students will do poorly, he can take a few weeks before test time to prepare them. In either case, tests need not strangle flexibility or creativity; they can be beaten.

Time and assistance, however, remain as obstacles, preventing teachers from developing their own materials and making the curricular decisions I spoke of earlier. The half-time teaching load I described in the Cardozo Project in Urban Teaching (two or three classes a day; half a day at elementary school) is costly yet some school systems reduce class loads for teachers who perform other school functions such as coaching, yearbook advising, and guidance. In addition to cost, what is really missing is the lack of will on the part of school authorities to take available dollars and convert platitudes about curriculum and teachers into realities. More

Effective Schools, launched by the United Federation of Teachers in New York, programed into each of the special schools planning time for teachers. Unfortunately, very little of that time was used to train teachers to develop instructional materials. Perhaps it will in the future.

But MES and the future do not speak to the classroom teacher in most inner-city schools. Time and assistance has yet to materialize. There are, however, compelling reasons for career teachers to squeeze out that twenty-fifth hour in the day and that last ounce of energy to develop and use their lessons and units: If they don't, intellectually they will die. Pride in performance and intellectual stimulation, as I pointed out in a previous chapter, are not encouraged by the organization of the school. In fact, the structure conspires against people thinking, interacting, and growing. To counteract this anti-intellectual cast of the school a teacher must decide to prepare materials for at least one class (if he is teaching junior or senior high students) or one content area in his elementary classroom. The next step, if a principal can be persuaded, is teaching a class with a colleague; next is team planning and cross-observations at a departmental or grade level (which, I feel, are just as fruitful and less threatening in the long run than team teaching. Whatever the process, the teacher has to do something to avoid intellectual atrophy.

Another reason is that if the thrust toward individualization of instruction pays off, someone has to program the materials that go into teaching machines and develop additional units for students to provide the diversity so necessary for individualization. Teachers are the logical candidates. But they must have time and training.

It is unfortunate that I urge teachers to bear the burden

for change when the university, with all its problems, expects and plans for intellectual performance from its staff through a reduced teaching load. My model for teaching, God forbid, is not the university scholar; it is the structural situation that permits teachers time, space, and assistance to develop their minds and eventually have it pay off in the classroom.

If a teacher does go through the process of developing curriculum materials then the question of how to present them—instruction—confronts him. I've stressed the unity of curriculum materials and instruction already and how each helps to shape the other. The next chapter deals with instruction in more detail.

Chapter V

Instruction

Effective instruction begins outside the classroom and inside the teacher's head. His perceptions and expectations about how youngsters will perform, his views of how the class should be organized and, most important, his ability to act upon these perceptions is where instruction and development of curriculum materials begin. Not exactly a profound observation, but unless their controlling influence is stressed, then the energy invested in spelling out strategies and tactics to shape and reshape those perceptions is wasted.

The influence of teachers' views, at least their negative

side, upon the performance of children was dealt with in Chapter 2. Evidence indicated that what a teacher believes about the race and class of his children colors not only his teaching style but also student achievement.

A sensitive layman has to spend only an hour with a teacher in class to sense how that teacher perceives his students. The tone of his voice (friendly, hostile, patronizing, etc.), his treatment of individual students (with or without respect, peremptory, condescending, listening attentively, etc.) —all signal the observer whether or not mutual respect exists. Rapport, that mystical word fondled lovingly by professional educators, implies a core of reciprocal respect; its presence or absence emerges from the teacher's perceptions and their subsequent implementation.

Thus, to exhort teachers to have respect for low-income students or to have them believe that poor, black children can learn as well as middle-class white ones is useless since it does not suggest specific actions to take and, more to the point, such exhortation is futile for those who already believe that black youngsters are not as capable as white ones or that poor children come from such nasty homes that there is little hope for their ever reaching "normal" achievement levels. Yet unconditional respect and the belief in the equal distribution of intelligence are two essential preconditions, among others, for effective instruction.

Because style and content of teaching stem, in large part, from perceptions, it is necessary to deal with them as early as possible for those planning to teach and immediately for those who now teach.[1] Much attention has been given re-

1. The problem of improving police performance with low-income ethnic groups is analogous in that a police officer's per-

cently to sensitivity training and other therapeutic techniques, phrases, by the way, that put teachers' teeth on edge as much as screeching chalk. There are numerous ways for individuals to examine their views and speak candidly about race, class, and themselves. Regardless of the means, unless adults who deal with children dredge up to the surface submerged assumptions and misconceptions for critical examination—a painful process to be sure—instruction will be scarred by blind, unquestioned "certainties" about children and one's self.

What examples I've used earlier have focused upon the hacks and bigots of both races who shamefully still staff classrooms. Few readers, however, would identify themselves as blatant racists. But there are other attitudes that can have an equally damaging effect upon children.

With the rediscovery of the poor in the early 60's, for example, thousands of well-intentioned whites—ranging from recent college graduates to suburban housewives—have begun teaching in "slum" schools. Many swallowed their fears generated by the horror stories they had heard and resolved to do something about inferior education. Others, unaware of such stories or ignoring them, entered classrooms on the strength of the moral fervor loosed by the Kennedy candidacy and administration. Armed with the belief that poor children needed a square deal, they marched into classrooms

---

ceptions about black people shape his behavior toward an individual Negro. The bitter cry of police brutality and demand for local control are responses toward the police department's past inability to train individual officers in differentiating among members of an ethnic group, understanding different styles of life, and recognizing fundamental similarities.

equipped with good intentions but little else. Within a few months, a year, perhaps two, most of them staggered out of the schools shaken and disillusioned.

Their disillusionment derived less from the stupidities of the system (although, Lord knows, they were in ample supply) but more from vague, unexamined attitudes and unrealistic expectations wedded to an enormous lack of instructional skills. Many of them entered the classroom believing that if the children were exposed to warm, compassionate adults who wanted them to learn, they would learn. Confronted by a range of behavior from apathy to belligerence, confronted by a bewildering and rich use of language, confronted by a school culture quite different (at least on first appearance) from their own, and confronted by a nagging guilt over whether or not racial feelings they discovered in themselves were valid—confronted by these awesome realities—many fine men and women retreated from the classroom. Many were overwhelmed by superficial differences in behavior. What does a teacher make out of an outburst in class between two strapping teenagers shouting "black motherfucker," "nigger," and "beat your ass" at each other? Awed by different styles of dress and language and lacking help from the school or university to make sense of these differences in terms of socio-economic status and possible cultural differences, a white teacher feels white and middle class and runs scared.

Another reaction to perceived differences besides fear is gushing compassion that drowns children in embraces and expressions like, "they're so cute," or for older youngsters, a suspension of all conventional expectations in performance. Excessive permissiveness, a mushy enthusiasm for the trivial, and an enormous lack of respect for the ability of students mark the liberal humanitarianism of some who have not explored their motives or feelings. More than a few white middle-class teachers, propelled by guilt, end up deluging their children in a sea of tears, used clothes, "A's" for minimal effort, and trips to the zoo. Just as inaccurate perceptions of poor children can lead to fear, so too can they produce a suffocating condescension regardless of the purest intentions. Thus, the full gamut of a teacher's perceptions and their influence upon what they expect of students must be part of any agenda to improve teaching in the inner-city.

Probably the most difficult knowledge to convey to teachers whose attitudes range from fear to condescension is how they often communicate these feelings without saying a word. Making teachers aware of non-verbal communication is a tough but essential task. After all, what means much more to kids is the deed not the word.

Few teachers are, for example, aware that how they arrange chairs and their desk either in the traditional front to back fashion or in a circle tells students more about the teacher's respect for student opinion than any number of pieties. Whether a teacher moves up and down the aisles or moves in and around student desks or whether the teacher sits at his desk most of the time again tells students clearly whether their teacher is or is not concerned about them. Whether teachers listen with both ears to a student, looking him full in the face, or whether the teacher continues to mark papers while the student is speaking, nodding occasionally and mumbling a few words periodically, signals respect or disrespect to the student. Curriculum materials on, say, Negro history, rock and roll music, or African literature send non-verbal messages to students that their interests are respected. Giving kids time to figure out for themselves solutions to problems tells them that the teacher respects their abilities. What teachers do and how they act are just as important as, if not more important than, what they say.

Turning to classroom organization, most teachers carry around in their heads the ideal vision of individualizing instruction—i.e., the teacher employing an arsenal of materials and a repertoire of methods that permit each student to operate to his fullest capacity. The vision—but not the reality—is renewed at faculty meetings and workshops, mainly through exhortation. Of course, most of the ideal is romantic nonsense since schools and teachers are singularly unprepared to deal with the intent or fullest meaning of individualizing instruction. The conventional public school operation cripples its implementation. In other words, each class in a building is taught as a group which is supposed to move uniformly from one topic to another except for occasional sub-groupings based upon tests and achievement. Any resemblance between individualizing of instruction and an average school is pure rhetoric. If instruction is to be effective, the organization of a classroom must be viewed by teachers on a continuum from learning in groups (large and small) to learning as individuals.[2] Such a view as opposed to the rigid lockstep movement of a whole class from one point to another requires a diversity of instructional techniques and materials. More

2. I favor those forms that crack the egg-crate mind set of administrators toward school organization; yet most of these points refer to a teacher and thirty or more students since team teaching, flexible scheduling, non-graded schools have yet to penetrate inner-city schools in a systematic manner. These suggestions, however, do contain the seeds of larger organizational forms.

important, when a classroom functions at different times as a large group, in small groups, and as individuals, all sorts of things will happen that come under the umbrella of learning as assuredly as a teacher leading a class in reciting the differences between *dig* and *dug*.[3]

Learning, obviously, is far more ecumenical than what has been traditionally defined by the school. What kids learn from one another and from the materials they use in a large- or small-group setting are just as valid as what they learn from a teacher. Viewing a class along the continuum I've suggested raises immediate questions about discipline which I will deal with later in the chapter. For the moment, I'm trying to stress the importance of seeing a group of children in flexible terms and not as a monolith that must be shoved from one predetermined step to the next.

None of this is new. I hesitate to write these words since educators say the same things again and again before and during a teacher's tenure in the classroom. They know that children do not learn the same thing at the same time; never have and never will. Even the finger-tip control teacher who can stare a class to attention knows very well that all are not listening, all are not functioning at the same level or same

3. As expected, the literature on grouping is mixed. Research findings on the benefits of homogeneous grouping as opposed to heterogeneous grouping cancel out one another. Grouping by ability is preferred by most teachers, once the pseudo reasons are sorted out, on the ground that it is easier to teach a class where the spectrum of ability difference is narrow. Whether ability grouping on the basis of paper and pencil tests facilitates learning, especially for inner-city children, is another issue. I feel that mixed grouping, while more demanding upon the teacher, provides students with the chance to learn from one another, thus tapping an additional source of learning experience.

speed. Seldom, however, do words combine with classroom experience to convert pieties into concrete possibilities.

Nor is what I have said about a broadened view of organizing a class innovative. Many teachers know in their guts that teaching thirty-five students the same thing at the same time only speaks to the pseudo administrative efficiency of a factory rather than of any superior learning results. The fact of the matter is that youngsters themselves are learning resources that can be tapped by classmates; kids can teach one another effectively. Seeing a class of thirty-five operating in a variety of groupings broadens the resources available in the class and multiplies the potential of both student and teacher. It isn't easy, however. In fact, it's damned hard.

Consider, for example, one facet of the difficulty that confronts those sharp, feeling-oriented middle-class men and women nourished on A. S. Neill's *Summerhill* and John Holt's books who decide to create at once Summerhillian or unstructured classrooms where freedom and creativity will flourish. In the first week rules are suspended and freedom reigns. Having immense faith in human potential irrespective of race or class, they are convinced that children must be freed immediately from the burdensome constraints of authority.

This is a recipe for disaster, and I've seen the disaster in classrooms where students use freedom as a club to intimidate classmates and harass the teacher; classrooms where license prevails. What is tragic about this failure is that these very capable young men and women analyze its origin inaccurately. Some believe that the system created youngsters that can't cope with freedom and responsibility (in part, a valid observation); others feel that the kids are really different—i.e., disturbed, troubled—and need a wholly separate form of education, such as is given the handicapped. A few, unfortunately, blame themselves. The analysis is often inaccurate since the type of classrooms that these people want is possible—indeed, they exist. The problem of creating these environments or any that depart from the traditional is a question of strategies, timing, and a great deal of skill and hard work.

CLASSROOM EXAMPLES

Some examples of classrooms at different points along the continuum follow.

Herbert Kohl, teaching for the first time in Harlem, described the unplanned development of an individualized reading program in his sixth-grade class. Many of the points made in the last chapter on learning style and curriculum also appear in this selection.

> I still stuck with the curriculum as much as possible. The social studies was impossible so I collected the books and returned them to the bookroom. It was too painful to see the children twist their faces into stupid indifference and hear their pained dull answers accompanied by nervous drumming on the desks.
>
> "New York is a large modern country."
>
> "The Hudson is an important ocean."
>
> "The Industrial Revolution was a benefit to all."
>
> Better drop it altogether, try anything so long as it didn't humiliate the children. These answers were not a function of the children's lack of experience, as the hopelessly respectable anti-poverty program believes; rather they were a direct response to the institutionalized hypocrisy that is characteristic of schools in the United States today.

I brought part of my library to school and temporarily substituted it for social studies. The children were curious about those Greeks and Latins who contributed so many words and concepts to our language. I brought in books on Greek and Roman architecture and art, as well as Robert Graves's version of the *Iliad,* a paperback translation of Apuleius' *Cupid* and *Psyche,* and *Larousse Encyclopedia* of *Mythology* and anything else that seemed relevant or interesting. I showed the books to the children and let them disappear into their desks. It was made clear that the books were to be read, and the pages to be turned. If someone reads a book so intensely that the book is bruised it is flattering to the book.

For three-quarters of an hour a day the Pantheon circulated along with Floyd Patterson and J. D. Salinger. Partridge's dictionary of word origins made its way through the class with Langston Hughes and the Bobbsey twins. Anything I could get my hands on was brought to class—a great deal remained unread and some books I hadn't read myself shocked and surprised the class. They were sexy and popular. Later that year my supervisor told me I was running a very effective individualized reading program. That may have been it, but the truth seemed simpler and less structured. I overwhelmed the class with books, many of which I loved, and let them discover for themselves what they liked. There were no reports to be written, no requirements about numbers of pages to be read. Some children hardly read at all, others devoured whatever was in the room. The same is true of my friends.

Robert Jackson grabbed a book on Greek architecture, copied floor plans and perspective drawings and, finally, leaping out of the book, created a reasonably accurate scale model of the Parthenon. Alvin and Michael built a clay volcano, asked for and got a chemistry book which showed them how to simulate an eruption. Sam, Thomas, and Dennis fought their way through war books; through the Navy, the Seabees, the Marines, and the Paratroops. The girls started with the Bobbsey twins and worked through to romantic novels and, in the case of a few, Thurber and O. Henry. I learned that there were no books to fear, and having been divested of my fear of idleness, I also wasn't worried if some children went through periods of being unable to do anything at all.

People entering my classroom during those forty-five minutes of "social" studies usually experienced an initial sense of disorder followed by surprise at the relative calm of the room. If they bothered to look more closely or ask, they would find that most of the children were working.

I remember once a supervisor from the District Office visited my class in late October. She entered the room unannounced, said nothing to me, but proceeded to ask the children what they were doing. In small groups or individually they showed her. She was pleased until she came to Ralph, who boldly told her that he was spending the morning ripping up pieces of paper—which is precisely what he had been doing all morning. Her whole impression of the classroom changed. I was a failure, allowing a child not to work, the thought of it . . . shocking. She took the situation into her own hands and spoke to Ralph. He merely turned a dumb face to her, rolled his eyes, and went back to his paper. She left, muttering something about discipline and emotional disturbance.

Ralph wasn't the only one who couldn't do anything for a while. When I started bringing books to school and opening the supply closets to the class, most children demurred from any change in routine. They wanted the social studies books even though they learned nothing from them; they enjoyed copying the mindless exercises that kept them dull and secure in class. It was just that I, as a teacher, couldn't pretend they were learning just to make our life together quieter and easier. So, with the textbooks gone many children stuck to chess and checkers. The girls started playing jacks, and with

> my encouragement created a vocabulary to describe the jack fever that seized them.[4]

Another time, Kohl described a class discussion with the 36 children.

> One day Ralph cursed at Michael and unexpectedly things came together for me. Michael was reading and stumbled several times. Ralph scornfully called out, "What's the matter, psyches, going to pieces again?" The class broke up and I jumped on that word "psyches."
>
> "Ralph, what does *psyches* mean?"
>
> An embarrassed silence.
>
> "Do you know how to spell it?"
>
> Alvin volunteered. "S-i-k-e-s."
>
> "Where do you think the word came from? Why did everybody laugh when you said it, Ralph?"
>
> "You know, Mr. Kohl, it means, like crazy or something."
>
> "Why? How do words get to mean what they do?"
>
> Samuel looked up at me and said: "Mr. Kohl, now you're asking questions like Alvin. There aren't any answers, you know that."
>
> "But there are. Sometimes by asking Alvin's kind of questions you discover the most unexpected things. Look."
>
> I wrote *Psyche,* then *Cupid,* on the blackboard. That's how *psyche* is spelled. It looks strange in English, but the word doesn't come from English. It's Greek. There's a letter in the Greek alphabet that comes out *psi* in English. This is the way *psyche* looks in Greek."
>
> Some of the children spontaneously took out their notebooks and copied the Greek.
>
> "The word *psyche* has a long history. *Psyche* means mind or soul for the Greeks, but it was also the name of a lovely woman who had the misfortune to fall in love with Cupid,

4. Reprinted by permission of the World Publishing Company from *36 Children* by Herbert Kohl. An NAL Book. Copyright © 1967 by Herbert Kohl.

the son of Venus, the jealous Greek goddess of love. . . ."

The children listened, enchanted by the myth, fascinated by the weaving of the meaning of *psyche* into the fabric of the story, and the character, Mind, playing tricks on itself, almost destroying its most valuable possessions through its perverse curiosity. . . .

I cited *psychological, psychic, psychotic, psychodrama, cupidity*—the children copied them unasked, demanded the meanings. They were obviously excited.

Leaping ahead, Alvin shouted: "You mean words change? People didn't always speak this way? Then how come the reader says there's a right way to talk and a wrong way?"

"There's a right way now, and that only means that's how most people would like to talk now, and how people write now."

Charles jumped out of his desk and spoke for the first time during the year.

"You mean one day the way we talk—you know, with words like *cool* and *dig* and *sound*—may be all right?"

"Uh huh. Language is alive, it's always changing, only sometimes it changes so slowly that we can't tell."

Neomia caught on.

"Mr. Kohl, is that why our readers sound so old-fashioned?"

And Ralph.

"Mr. Kohl, when I called Michael *psyches,* was I creating something new?"

Someone spoke for the whole class.

"Mr. Kohl, can't we study the language we're talking about instead of spelling and grammar? They won't be any good when language changes anyway."

We could and we did. That day we began what had to be called for my conservative plan book "vocabulary," and "an enrichment activity."[5]

5. *Ibid.,* pp. 23–24.

In my "slow-learner" U.S. History classes, eleventh graders were often asked to work in groups. In studying slavery in the American South, for example, six teams of students spent two days each sorting out a long list of laws taken from slave codes of two countries. Those laws that were part of the southern slave code (students had read at length from documents of slaves and masters) had to be separated from those laws that were part of an unnamed country's slave code. There were enough differences in the list of laws for students to pick up clues and do the categorizing, but not too many to make it self-evident or another busy-work exercise. Thus, within each team spirited debate arose about where each law belonged. After a group reached a consensus, each law was cut out of the list and pasted on cards marked American South and Country X. The decision was important since the teams were competing against one another for points to be awarded on how accurately the laws were categorized. Yet the competition was not that lethal sort often seen in classrooms where particular students often end up humiliated; although it was a gimmick, it rapidly developed into an intriguing intellectual task.

My role was that of a resource person. When questions arose over the meaning of a particular law I would clarify or elaborate. In short, students didn't depend upon me for information, discipline, or direction.

In another class, the complete continuum of structured-to-unstructured classroom organization developed, much of it out of students' suggestions. In the aftermath of Dr. Martin Luther King's assassination and the eruption of protest and rioting in Washington, D.C., including the area where I taught, members of the class asked if we could study white attitudes or as one student put it, "I'm tired of being studied."

Building upon what the class had studied of white attitudes in antebellum America, I prepared materials on attitudes in the 1930's and 1950's for the students to read and discuss as a class. When we finished, I asked about white feelings today. I mentioned some polls. Some students, however, went to great lengths and into great detail to extract from their experiences evidence that white racism was just as virulent today as it was in the past. The Kerner Report, which the class was aware of, only confirmed what they felt. Still there was enough doubt to prompt some students to ask about white people in Washington and their attitudes toward the rioting and, more specifically, toward the poor in the ghetto. I suggested a survey of opinion and the class liked the idea.

Statements on which people could agree or disagree were drawn up by three students and myself. The next day the three of them presented the list to the class and spent the period enlarging the initial pool of statements. I sat in the back of the class offering suggestions and trying, unsuccessfully at times, to keep my mouth shut. Two students volunteered to type up the statements on ditto masters; I duplicated them and copies of the survey were given to the class to begin the poll the next day. A problem arose. One student asked how truthful would white people be to a black interviewer, especially a teenager. A good question. This point produced a spirited discussion on whether the results of a poll are influenced by the race of the pollster. Out of this, came three suggestions, none of which I had anticipated. In addition to white people polled by the class, the group decided that the survey should be administered to black people; furthermore, the survey should be given by white students to white people;

and finally, names should be picked randomly from the suburban telephone book. Thus three checks were established to neutralize their hunches about the race of pollsters influencing the results. Validating the hunches would depend upon the information turned up by other interviewers and mailed responses.

After arrangements were made, four periods were spent in conducting the survey during school hours, in addition to the time some students spent in polling white shoppers in the suburbs. When the surveys were turned in, the results were tallied, arrangements with the white students were completed, and copies to suburbanites were sent out. What happened during this week was that the students worked in self-selected groups completing each of the tasks. I helped each of the groups—i.e., tallying, licking stamps, making phone calls, and so on. Over a two-week period, we met as a class twice. The remainder of the time was taken up with small-group activity, individuals or pairs working. Not all the students pitched in; a few played around for the two-week period; one or two did nothing, proving, I guess, that there is nothing magical about a particular organizational form.

What is really important here is not the number of kids who didn't fully participate or whether the sample population polled was accurate or whether the conclusions reached by the class on the results of the poll stacked up against recent research; the importance lay in the process of creating, administering, and tallying a poll and measuring its results against the hunches kids had about white attitudes. In other words, an organizational device tapped student resources in teaching skills and knowledge.

The diversity of classroom organization permitted the

aims of this survey to be fulfilled, whereas a conventional classroom scheme completely dominated by the teacher could have aborted the plan.

Again, at the risk of being repetitious, what Kohl did, what happened in my class, and what occurs in other rooms depends to a large degree upon not getting locked into conventional, structured, whole-class instruction. Notice, however, that classroom organization is intimately tied up with who the person is, his relationship with the kids, and the materials and teaching strategies he uses in the classroom.

THE BOGEYMAN

Instruction, then, begins outside the classroom in the attitudes, expectations, and plans of the teachers. But once inside the classroom, the best of intentions, the noblest of concerns, and the sharpest of lessons are paralyzed by the bogeyman of discipline. When the door closes, the vocabulary of what educators call euphemistically "classroom management" takes over: conformity—control—authority—structure—tight ship —routines.

Yet to the problem of discipline, like the suggestions for diversity in classroom organization, the same caveats must be raised. Just as there is nothing intrinsically magical about knowing the mechanics of small-group, large-group, and individual instruction, so there is nothing mystical about knowing rules for controlling kids. While a shopping list of rules may soothe administrators into thinking that teachers will perform well once the list is memorized, rules do little for the individual teacher who must learn about children and his personal strengths and weaknesses before applying those formulas. Nevertheless, a separate body of literature written by veteran teachers and principals—a sociology of classroom control—has gained wide appeal.

Consider the following portion of an article which appeared in a professional journal for educators and is probably one of the better examples of concrete advice on discipline to teachers of the "disadvantaged."

> "Unruly" students are considered the norm among disadvantaged youngsters. Those who are given special help often return to the classroom as difficult as ever. The problem of discipline is acute and in most ghetto schools is the number one problem for the teacher. Pat rules of discipline and teaching are discarded. Teachers resort to methods not prescribed or condoned by the book if they are considered practical and effective; good teaching in many ghetto schools really means good discipline. . . .
>
> Disadvantaged children are not naturally "bad" in class. They want to learn and can be taught, as long as the teacher does not lose his confidence or surrender his authority. With any group of children, a teacher's authority will be tested immediately, and possibly thereafter, depending on how he handles himself and the class. The students who are testing the teacher hope he will not find out what they are doing, or hope he will not be able to cope with them. But if the teacher ignores them or indicates that he is helpless, they will feel insecure and lose their respect for him. The other children in the class are watching and hoping that the teacher will handle the situation properly. If he fails them, they will try to reject and eventually turn against him.
>
> The teacher, then, must learn to solve his own classroom problems. The dean or guidance counselor is usually too overburdened to mete out punishment for every "problem" child. The classroom is the teacher's fortress [sic] and the students must be made to realize this important fact.
>
> To what extent the teacher is successful will largely de-

pend on his classroom management; that is, the rules and routine he establishes with his students. In middle-class schools it is possible to get along without good classroom management, but in ghetto schools it is not. Faced individually, most disadvantaged children are very friendly, but in a class situation the relationship can change radically. They are restless and impulsive. They cannot tolerate waiting and have a voracious desire for excitement. They are easily disconcerted and "fly off the handle." The teacher, therefore, establishes order and routine immediately, before he attempts to teach, so the children know what to do and what is expected of them.

A disadvantaged child in junior high school is perhaps the most difficult to deal with. By then, many students are rebellious and too retarded in basic skills to learn in a regular classroom situation. Many are strong enough to be a physical threat or sophisticated enough to probe a teacher's weak points. But they are not mature enough to reason with or old enough to be legally expelled if they really become "problems." These children especially require a strict, structured, workable routine. They need and want a teacher who can assure them the stability they usually do not receive at home.

The child should understand that the reasons for rules and routine, which should be made clear, have a definite purpose and be ordered around the viewpoint that the teacher and the class are working together and that any discord or breach of this mutual endeavor [is] a waste of time. Some of the rules to be examined seem almost too basic for explanation. Yet my experience is that they are far from rudimentary. Although they can apply to any group of students, they *should* [original italics] be used with the disadvantaged and varied only slightly to suit each teacher.

[Explanations follow each rule. I have omitted some and retained others wherever they dealt with discipline. I have also retained some of the fuller explanations to give the flavor and intent of certain rules.]

- Train your students to enter the room in an orderly fashion. . . .
- Keep a clean and attractive room. . . .
- Be certain you have everybody's attention before you start the lesson. . . .
- Be consistent with your class routine.

These children cannot cope with change. The place reserved on the blackboard for homework, the date, and the aim of the lesson should not be changed. Changes should be gradual and infrequent.

- Get to know students early in the term. . . .
- Hold students accountable.

Challenge the student who comes late or does not do his homework. Make him an example, but never humiliate him. Make sure he understands that his grade is affected by everything he does in class. Do not let anything go unnoticed if you can possibly help it. The children will soon realize that they cannot get away with poor preparation or behavior.

- Speak softly. . . .
- Be clear with your instructions. . . .
- Aim to have full class participation. . . .
- Be aware of undercurrents of behavior.

Reserve part of your attention while instructing to watch, look and listen. Do not become so absorbed in the lesson that you lose audience contact. Do not fix your eyes on the child who is reciting. Take note of everyone's work. Avoid trouble by anticipating trouble. Call on a disruptive child to answer questions or to go to the blackboard. Try not to turn your back to the class, especially for any great length of time. . . .

- Keep the pupils in their seats.

Keep students from getting out of their seats, and most of your serious discipline problems will be reduced. Do not permit indiscriminate walking or wandering about. This creates an opportunity for one child to poke or punch another child, a "sport" the disadvantaged child often enjoys. . . . Similarly, do not allow students to come to your desk to ask questions, it may lead to confusion on your part. Permit only one student to stand at a time. Keep a record of those who use the pass for any "emergency.". . .

- Depend on interest to maintain order. . . .
- Be friendly but maintain a proper distance.

Be willing to play the marginal role of entertainer. Be willing to ride a wave; namely, take a joke or else the children will try to make more waves. However, never become too friendly. The children will take advantage. Similarly, never descend to their level [sic]. The children prefer to keep the teacher on a different plane.

- Be consistent with discipline. . . .
- Be flexible. . . .
- Use good judgment. . . .
- Always work with the individual offender. . . .
- Handle all disciplinary cases yourself whenever possible. . . .
- Take immediate action whenever events call for it. . . .
- Apply restraint, keep calm. . . .
- Do not make the offense personal, do not allow audience situations. . . .
- Be certain to dismiss the class.

When teaching disadvantaged children it is of paramount importance to understand them—who they are, how they live, and what they want. The teacher also needs "common sense," something he cannot learn from books or practice teaching. . . . He should cope with and transfer their frustrations and anger, of which they have a great deal, to constructive purposes. . . .[6]

6. Allan C. Ornstein, "Teaching the Disadvantaged," *Educational Forum,* January, 1967, pp. 215–223. Used by permission of Kappa Delta Pi Honor Society in Education.

Surveying veteran teachers of inner-city schools on the validity of these rules would, I think, reveal a consensus of agreement. Stripped of sentimentality, they might say, here is the practical side of day-to-day teaching. No rhetoric. No platitudes. No preaching. This is the way it is.

It is this way and will continue to be so if such advice is adopted uncritically. Consider, for example, the sort of model teacher that emerges after executing every last rule to perfection. Maybe a kindly Marine platoon sergeant or a benign prison guard? The language of the advice implies fear of a volatile enemy; the metaphor is the military; the strategy is containment. And it is important to understand this. The ideal teacher, according to the internal logic of the suggestions, enforces silence and demands conformity. Not exactly the image that would attract sensitive and concerned teaching candidates to inner-city schools, yet this, veterans would sharply reply, is reality.

It is and it isn't. So much is left unsaid in such advice that the reader doesn't know if "disadvantaged" kids are basically "unruly," "restless," and "impulsive" as Ornstein suggests or if they behave in the manner he and others describe because of the way the school and teachers structure their environment. Seldom do teachers and educators who dispense cookbook recipes for orderly classrooms concern themselves with why kids behave the way they do. If new forms are to be created in inner-city classrooms, the *why* is crucial. Instead of asking this question, a teacher's energy is devoted to maintaining order rather than addressing himself to the real task of teaching skills and knowledge.

By not asking why kids behave in school as they do, educators inevitably miss the distinction between tactics, strategies, and goals. Tactics, in this instance, the shopping list of rules, should be part of an overall strategy that includes other means of achieving certain goals, say, an independent thinking youngster who can cope with an ever-changing world. The narrow tactics of containment, sadly, has become the goal. Primitive forms of maintaining order are used to teach youngsters discipline. And if they don't learn to control themselves and listen to the teacher, then even cruder tactics are used—all geared to teach youngsters to conform and not to think or question.

Furthermore, notice that all the advice pertains to whole-class (25–40 students) instruction. Given the language used to describe kids, to consider teaching and learning through small-group and individual processes would be unthinkable. Unpredictable things might happen and unpredictablity in the classroom struggle for power is to be avoided. Because of the schoolman's mind-set upon whole-group instruction, discipline continues as *the* massive obstacle for inner-city teachers to overcome; little attention is directed toward small-group and individual instruction which demand organizational skills but where management issues diminish to zero.

Although I criticize how-to-do-it lists because they frame a classroom in terms of a prison or a military campaign and subvert the goals of instruction and curriculum, many of the specific techniques—once learned and used with judgment—are, paradoxically, essential for initial survival in inner-city classrooms. In authoritarian schools, where beliefs that students have enormous intellectual, emotional, and cultural shortcomings merge with an intrinsic lack of faith in youth, such devices are necessary if a teacher intends to last beyond Thanksgiving, mainly because children come to share those beliefs and that faith.

The techniques of managing a large class of youngsters

are of critical importance to the new teacher for one reason: Students (as early as the second grade) have strong expectations about how teachers should teach, how classrooms should be organized, and what learning is.

These expectations, regardless of how conservative they are, should be accommodated to and eventually changed. Ignore them and the chances of building firm relationships with children and teaching effectively are reduced.

STUDENT EXPECTATIONS

A word on student expectations.[7] Often overlooked, student views have a powerful effect upon behavior, as assuredly as teacher expectations. Students as well as teachers have a mind-set on student types, classroom organization, and the like, and carry around perceptions about them. Regardless of how naive or short-sighted they may appear to be, student feelings in these matters must be recognized, accepted, accommodated to initially, and changed.

Students, for example, expect a teacher to lay down rules, hand out texts, demand silence, and assign homework—in short, to run a tight ship. These expectations don't preclude students testing the limits of the teacher's ability to enforce the rules; it is part of the early trading off that marks the

7. The Coleman Report and *Racial Isolation in the Public Schools,* published by the U.S. Commission on Civil Rights, underscored the collective influence of attitudes and behavior when ethnic low-income youngsters form the majority of students. The cumulative influence of peer attitudes and behavior, according to the reports, is the single most important variable influencing achievement. Another strong influence on achievement was the caliber of the teacher. There is some evidence that teachers make a difference.

struggle between teacher and class. If the teacher uses the techniques of control satisfactorily while simultaneously proving to children that he can teach, the class will settle into a routine comfortable to them. But if the teacher cannot conform to their expectations or has strong doubts about his use of authority, then clever minds click, strategies change, and tactics shift: another teacher, regardless of his goodwill, exits crying, cursing, and totally exhausted.

Veteran teachers and principals recognize the difficulties new teachers face in taking hold with a class and invariably inform newcomers what to do the first few weeks in much the same language as Ornstein uses. What often happens, sadly, is that many teachers, not fully knowing themselves, get trapped by such advice: get trapped by the devices they use and get trapped by student expectations.

So often temporary measures harden into permanence. A teacher-dominated, one-way communication system in the Fall often sputters to an incoherent end in June. James Herndon's *The Way It Spozed To Be* describes how students burst out in the Spring from those classes whose teachers prided themselves on rules, routines, and discipline.

The balance of power in a classroom is so fragile; teachers seldom wish to jeopardize an uneasy truce by changing tactics between September and June. Thus, the trap. What teachers must learn is to adapt the shopping list of rules to their personality and use them as tools to gain the respect of youngsters; then, still preserving the relationship, re-fashion with those very same tools and additional ones, the old forms to redefine limits, learning, and teacher-student interactions.[8]

8. Some may question this strategy and prefer to start from scratch with a new order of things in September, that is, disregard-

A few examples are in order. Most teachers and educators emphasize the "disadvantaged's" need for structure, a framework of rules and routines for kids to operate within. In most cases this "need" for structure is linked to the concept of a culture of poverty or the general instability of poor families. Inflated to critical importance, rules and routines become ends in themselves, leading some school officials in Washington, D.C., a few years ago, but since rescinded, to order compulsory attendance for all male students in the cadet corps because most of the students who were black and poor needed the stability of military procedures. How's that for a bastardized sociology?

Yet among the many by-products of Head Start, Upward Bound, and the Job Corps was the plain fact that poor youths could operate in both structured and unstructured settings. More to the point, go into the plushest suburban elementary schools and ask teachers about structure for their children. In most instances, they will tell you of the child's need for rules and the importance of order to children being socialized

---

ing student expectations. I've seen this work with well-integrated, strong teachers who had a high tolerance for initial disorder and student resistance. Ignoring the influence of student perceptions increases the risk of failure in the conventional school setting, but gambles for the sweet possibility of a real success in terms of student growth which, in my opinion, can go further than the strategy of meeting student expectations from the onset. I recommend what is essentially a conservative approach because it requires the least change from students initially and maximizes the chances of new teachers gaining that degree of confidence in themselves necessary to make eventual changes. (For what happens when teacher and student expectations are ignored and multiple innovations are introduced, read Paul Lauter's "The Short, Happy Life of Adams-Morgan," *Harvard Education Review,* Spring, 1968, pp. 235–262.

as responsible citizens. No social science excuses about the instability of the family, although the father may be just as absent albeit for different reasons.

Stripping away the excuses, structure is important not because of poverty or affluence, absent fathers or working mothers, intrinsic or extrinsic needs; it is important in so far as it meets students' expectations and establishes the ground rules for communication between teacher and class and among students.

There are many structures. Some inhibit, others encourage interaction. One form, for example, is the tight-ship framework. Rules are clearly explained and firmly but fairly enforced. Established routines permit tasks to be performed with speed and efficiency. Each student knows precisely what is expected of him at any given point. If the teacher is capable, students are comfortable with this form since it requires of them little more than passive acquiescence; teachers are comfortable with this form since all authority, decision-making, and wisdom flow from them. Communication is usually one-way with a minimum of feedback from the children.

Unless changes to maximize interaction are introduced by the teacher, this form hardens into rigidity, inhibiting the child's growth in independence and thinking skills. Furthermore, communication reduces itself to a one-way trickle of orders, "suggestions," and reprimands. It does not have to be so.

If the teacher understands the utility of different structures, then diverse learning situations can be gradually introduced. For competitive purposes the class can be broken into groups, for example, to seek answers to problems deriving from the content studied, to search out information, or for any number of reasons. More individualized work can be planned around an assortment of instructional materials where student choices count. Such learning situations often have to be introduced by the teacher since youngsters have had either very little experience with diverse settings or only some slight exposure to them, and these usually have been teacher-dominated and involved no real training. Once children gain skills in working together and once they realize the teacher is sincere in pursuing it seriously as an alternative for them to choose among, multiple-learning situations become commonplace experiences for low-income youngsters.

Just as necessary are mechanisms that permit youngsters to voice disagreement, suggest changes, and make decisions so that by the end of the school year what began as a "tight ship" has been transformed into a more flexible framework of learning in which students play an active role in shaping what happens in the classroom.

All of this is to say that a structure is another tool, not an end product; that to be effective a teacher should establish a form that meets the students' expectations, gains their respect, and then transcends those expectations by creating different ones which open up a real interaction between and among teacher and students. Like all suggested teaching strategies, meeting student perceptions and going beyond them is easy to recommend; but implementation—the real payoff—depends upon individual judgment, personal qualities of the teacher, and firsthand experiences with veteran practitioners who are successful at it.

In *The Culturally Deprived Child,* Frank Riessman described an effective teacher. I've selected those portions of the description that deal with discipline. The specific, very concrete advice offered deals with the elementary school but it applies as well to secondary level students. Compare the earlier advice of Ornstein with this. Notice the similarities in specific points but differences in tone.

> Miss L. told us she starts her first class with a full question-and-answer discussion of what she calls the ground rules of the course. She begins:
>
> "You and I are going to live together for the next year. To get along, what will we have to do? What problems will we have to face and how can we handle them?" In the course of this first meeting she states:
>
> "I am here to teach; you are here to learn. I want to tell what I can do to help you. Now, to do this we need some rules." She then asks them to discuss why certain rules, such as "no running in class," are necessary. During the hour some child will usually raise his hand and ask whether he can get a drink of water. In response she says, "You're too old to *ask* for water; *tell me* you want a drink and unless I need you here that very minute it will be OK with me if you go."
>
> Another thing that happens every opening day is the "initiation" of the teacher. "This is a highly organized, cooperative effort to break the new teacher. They want to see how smart you are, how much you can stand. So one child says it's too light in the room—can we pull down the shades. Then another one complains it's too dark—can we pull them up. Somebody else is too warm and wants the windows open, while still another party is too cold. This is a game the kids love to play."
>
> And what is the teacher supposed to do, we asked? "Stand firm, show that you're wise to the game, kid about it, but don't go along with it. You are the master of the ship and you will decide when it's too cold, too light, and so on. Always remember the class is your fortress [sic]."
>
> After about three weeks the class has a period of mutual evaluation in which they discuss how well the teacher has

been living up to her part of the bargain, and vice versa. Some child may tell her that she hasn't paid enough attention to some other child. When the criticisms are accurate, "and they often are," she accepts them and tries to correct the situation. The children learn soon enough that they can depend on her, that she will stand by what she says. For example, one day the teacher stated that a news story appearing in the *New York Daily News* was also in the *New York Times.* The children said it wasn't. Miss L. replied that she would eat the newspaper if it wasn't in the *Times,* because she was so dead sure she was right. The following day she discovered that she had been wrong, whereupon she obtained a cake from the school cafeteria, stuffed the newspaper inside of it, and ate it in front of the entire class. . . .

We asked Miss L. what she did when the rules were disobeyed. "I never have them clean the board or anything like that as punishment. We all share in cleaning up and it isn't a punishment. Nor do I give them a learning assignment to do because a punishment should simply be a waste of time, and should not be confused with learning. What I do is merely give them a great many foolish sentences to write, read them carefully to check they have done them correctly and then tear them up and throw them away. I want them to realize that the task is just a waste of time. If the situation is very serious, I call up the parents and explain to them in front of the child that he is not letting me teach him. But I don't call the parents just when something goes wrong. I try to call them everytime the child does something especially delightful, and so I have a basic contact with them. . . .

"Another thing about discipline—when I apply the rules, I never get indignant and I don't humiliate the child. The rules are purely objective and I'm only 'sorry' that they have violated them and therefore require punishment. I get the children to realize that all of us have to accept the consequences of our behavior. And I repeat over and over again that breaking the rules means 'I can't teach you, I can only think that you do not want to learn.' Of course, punishment and threats should be rare—you shouldn't have to punish children often. It's more of a last resort and loses its meaning if it becomes habitual. For most common occurrences, I am more prone to say to the disobeying child, 'You are letting me down—you're breaking our agreement.' One thing is certain, these kids want limits. It's time we get over the idea that discipline means rigidity and dictatorship. The deprived child thrives on rules and order and if he respects and likes you, he hasn't the least desire to rebel. He wants you to be firm, but responsive. Firmness doesn't mean brutality or hardness. To brutality he responds in kind, and then the classroom becomes a jungle. . . .

"Authority and discipline go hand in hand. And authority has to be developed day by day, through clear statements and application of rules and regulations and lots of repetition."

What do you do, we asked, when a child gets angry at you and actually rebels?

"Oh, a child will sometimes say 'Who do you think you are?' I answer with all the dignity I can muster, 'I am *your teacher*.' And if a child threatens to hit me. I say, 'I don't think you'd do a thing like that—I am your teacher.' Usually, if the children are behaving this way, they need more exercise. I find that a very good practice is to have the children take fairly frequent breaks during which they do calisthenics and deep breathing. This lets off a lot of steam, gives them some fresh air, and relaxes them. Breaks are also particularly good because, in the early transition to the school, they are not used to paying attention for long periods of time."

We then queried Miss L. on what she did when the children used vile language.

"Mainly roll with the punches, never get flabbergasted, show that you know the lingo, and are not 'stuck up.' Answer or deal with whatever they have said irrespective of the language, and then, as sort of an afterthought, remark that 'we do not use that kind of language in this class, please.' And don't think I haven't gotten unrequested apologies, sometimes as much as a week later."

How about fighting—what do you do about that, we asked? "I make it perfectly clear that I have nothing against fighting, that it's OK to know how to defend yourself, but in my classroom I can't teach you if there are going to be fisticuffs. If a fight is already in progress, I very often ask the two or three biggest boys in the class to help break it up—if they are not already involved in it, that is. Or sometimes I tap one of the combatants on the shoulder and ask if he has a match."[9]

Miss L. is firm. She consults her students and listens to what they have to say. Chances are that she becomes more flexible as the year progresses. Yet here is only one teaching style among many. Herbert Kohl, John Holt, Jonathan Kozol, my colleagues, your best high school teacher, and I, differ in manner one from the other in maintaining a cooperative classroom climate. Diverse teaching styles rule out a single way of managing a class and following a shopping list of sure-fire prescriptions.

Having said that in no way dispels the bogeyman of discipline from the minds of teachers in inner-city classrooms. If management of a class is so inextricably a part of a teacher's personality, organizational skills, materials, and instructional techniques, then the best I could do is cast the issue of classroom management into a larger arena, focusing upon its instrumental value and not viewing it as a barrier to be breached and held on to for dear life. I cannot drive away the

9. From pp. 89–93, *The Culturally Deprived Child,* by Frank Riessman. Copyright © 1962 by Frank Riessman. Reprinted by permission of Harper and Row, Publishers.

phantom of discipline. Supervised classroom experience where an individual can learn about himself and work out the hang-ups common to newcomers is far more useful than words.

GETTING DOWN TO METHODS: TEACHING STRATEGIES

For some irritated readers, the substance of instruction (or methodology) doesn't seem to be on the agenda. To explain, clarify, and analyze information—the traditional meaning of instruction, and all very essential components—are part of a larger definition that I prefer: instruction is anything performed or used by the teacher and student directed toward learning specific skills, knowledge, and attitudes. Again, curriculum and instruction converge.

Although I offer a rough definition, I hold out no theory of instruction for the "disadvantaged." Any comprehensive statement must be embedded within a solid foundation of how children learn; as I read the literature, there is still a great deal that adults have to understand about the ways of kids. To put it abrasively, John Holt's brilliant mapping out of the school terrain says more, in my opinion, about how chilldren do, and do not, learn than educators steeped in the latest research. Yet, so much more has to be mapped out. Much of what I have to say, then, deals with instruction in a primitive way; less of the cookbook is here and more of some general teaching strategies.

Methodology as a topic raises some vexing problems. The controversy over learning to read suggests a few parallels for discussing teaching strategies for low-income youngsters.

Jeanne Chall in *Learning to Read: The Great Debate* surveyed exhaustively the methods of teaching children to read from 1910 to 1965. Examining the ideologies behind phonics (or teaching kids to break the code) and "look-say" (or teaching for meaning), reviewing the research on these and related methods, visiting classrooms, interviewing educators and academicians, analyzing the instructional materials, Chall concluded somewhat discouragingly that:

> One of the most important things, if not *the* most important thing, I learned from studying the existing research on beginning reading is that it says nothing consistently. . . . And if you select judiciously and avoid interpretations you can make the research "prove" almost anything you want it to.
>
> How interested people are in learning to read [a crucial concern of methodology], I concluded, is not determined by what method or set of materials they are using. Generally, it is *what the teacher did* [original italics] with the method, the materials and the children rather than the method itself that seemed to make the difference. . . .[10]

She did find, however, that one approach, code emphasis, was better than others for beginning readers. Her comments on methods, in general, deserve quoting.

> My belief that the choice of . . . [teaching beginning reading by breaking the code] does not lessen in any way my conviction about the importance of good teaching. Indeed, as we learn more about the teaching of beginning reading, we may find a poor method in the hands of a good teacher producing better results than a good method in the hands of

10. Jeanne Chall, *Learning to Read: The Great Debate* (New York: McGraw-Hill, 1967), p. 87.

> a poor teacher. But this is not the point. . . . Good teaching is always needed. But a good method in the hands of a good teacher—that is the ideal. . . .

Although the word "good" is fuzzy, Chall restates an old maxim: There are no good or bad methods; only good or bad outcomes. Turning to the "disadvantaged," is there a teaching strategy that clearly stimulates interest, produces higher achievement, and engenders positive attitudes? In view of the impressive array of evidence on home and peer influences, probably not.

Chall found herself in a similar predicament. The ongoing debate failed to reveal clear prescriptions for success in the teaching of reading. Much depended upon the teacher, material, child, and method. Still, she did conclude, qualifications and all, that one cluster of approaches—i.e., code emphasis—should be employed more than look-say methods for beginning reading. Similarly, there are some approaches that should be used with low-income youngsters more so than other approaches. Why? What is the evidence?

There is virtually none. Evaluation of school performance based upon a particular teaching strategy is in its primitive stages. And if one accepts the data uncovered by the Office of Education's study on Equality of Educational Opportunity (the Coleman Report), little if anything that the school does matters insofar as raising student achievement is concerned. In this instance, I disagree.

On what basis, then, can I argue for a particular teaching strategy applicable to poor kids, a group that I stress is highly diversified? My reasons would be, I fear, unacceptable to academicians since they contain no rigorous samples, control groups, regression analysis; in other words, no "hard" data. It is all "soft." Unburdened by a research apparatus, the best I can offer are strong hunches based upon firsthand experiences.

That in 1969 a reasonable intelligent teacher with twelve years in the classroom can only fall back upon experience speaks to the paucity of operational knowledge among educators and, perhaps, to the inability of researchers to communicate their findings to practitioners like myself in an intelligent manner. There is, fortunately, a small but growing body of opinion on how low-income children should be taught, although its implications for all children are self-evident. Much of it has been written by teachers and sensitive academicians who wisely went into classrooms to watch and listen to children and teachers. Research has yet to build a solid base of evidence for their insights. Until that foundation is built, I must go with what I feel works. And what I think works is using techniques and materials that exploit the learning styles of youngsters, roughly sketched out in the last chapter, tapping their interests and concerns and parlaying them into a larger teaching strategy.

Part of that teaching strategy is taking the elements of curriculum materials (emphasis on people, concreteness, conflict, and relevance) and shaping instructional techniques from them. The following description of a class depicts their use in a junior high school English class.

> In Syracuse, New York, Madison Junior High possesses all the grim indices of poverty and educational disadvantages. [The school has since been closed down.] The teacher wanted his English class to know that there are a variety of language styles, each in itself valid but still used for dif-

ferent purposes. He chose the following Langston Hughes poem to kick off the class.

> I play it cool and dig all jive.
> That's the reason I stay alive.
> My motto, as I live and learn,
> Is: dig and be dug in return.

After the students read the poem, there was a long moment of silence. Then came the exclamations.

"Hey, this is tough."

"Hey, Mr. Weinstein, this cat is pretty cool."

"It's written in our talk."

But when asked the meaning of "playing it cool," the students had difficulty verbalizing the idea.

A boy volunteered to act it out.

Weinstein took the part of a teacher and the boy pretended he was walking down the hallway.

"Hey you," said the teacher, "you're on the wrong side of the hall. Get over where you belong."

Without looking up, the boy calmly and slowly walked to the other side and continued without any indication of what was going on his mind.

That was "playing it cool."

When Weinstein asked a boy to show what he would do when not playing it cool, a verbal battle ensued.

The class began offering definitions for "playing it cool"; calm, collected, no strain.

Weinstein suggested another, "nonchalant." A new word.

Next came a discussion of the phrase "dig all jive."

One student told how he once got into trouble because he didn't "dig the jive" of a group of streetcorner toughs.

So the message of Hughes' poem, the class discovered, was that he "stayed alive" because he "dug all jive"—understood all kinds of talk.

Hughes' motto was to "dig and be dug in return"—understand and be understood.

> The students were amazed at their own analysis.
>
> Weinstein asked the students how many kinds of jive they understood. Why all kinds, of course.
>
> [Mr. Weinstein] launched into an abstract [lecture] on the nature of truth using all the big words he could find.
>
> The students looked blank.
>
> He then asked them to test his understanding of their jive. They threw colloquialisms at him and he got five out of six.
>
> The class was impressed.
>
> "According to Hughes," Weinstein asked, "who has the better chance of staying alive, you or I?"
>
> "The jive you have mastered is a beautiful one," Weinstein said. "But you have to dig the school jive too, the jive that will occur in other situations. That's what school is for, to help you dig all jive and stay alive."[11]

In this lesson, the teaching strategy hit the learning style through role-playing of teacher and student; the experiences of kids through discussion of the students' language; and one particular concern of youngsters in discussing language's relationship to success in the adult world. The content of the lesson (Langston Hughes' poem and the necessity of knowing different languages), the techniques used (role-playing and much interactive discussion) contain an emphasis on people, concreteness, conflict, and relevance that—I feel—should mark a teaching strategy for children in inner-city schools.

Look for these four elements in the following U.S. History class dealing with the topic of slavery as a cause of the Civil War.

> "Let's look at this, class," the teacher began. "Less than ten percent of Southern whites owned slaves, but they all

11. Frank Riessman, "Teachers of the Poor: A Five Point Plan," presented at Syracuse University Conference on Urban Education and Cultural Deprivation, July 15–16, 1964.

fought for slavery. How could the ten percent persuade the ninety percent who didn't own slaves to fight for them?"

Turning to two girls and a boy seated at his extreme right, he says,

"You're the slave owners. The rest of the class and I don't own slaves. Persuade us to fight for you."

One girl, giggling, tries:

"These Yankees, they want to come down and take everything away from you."

"Oh, no, they don't," the teacher says. "Just from you. I'm just a poor dirt farmer. I don't have anything they want."
"Our whole economy is based upon slaves," says one slaveholder.

"No, sir," says a boy in the non-slave-holding section, falling into the spirit of the situation. "My economy isn't. I got to do my own work."

The debate rages for a while; when it lagged, the teacher interjected.

"Come on, now; why will these eight million whites fight for four years? If you can't come up with this, class, the whole thing is completely unreal. Just something in a textbook."

Finally, in the heat of the argument, one of the Negro girls in the slaveholding section comes up with,

"Remember those slave rebellions? Remember what happened on those plantations? The Yankees will come down here and raise up those Negroes to be *your equals,* and there'll be no controlling them."

The class roars with laughter at her and she bends her head.

But they sense the truth of what she's said.

"Let's give it a name," the teacher says. He writes on the board, "*White Supremacy.*" He asks, "Anyone come across U. B. Phillips in the readings I gave you?"

One boy has read something by him and says, "He thinks that's the whole theme of Southern History."

The one white boy in the class, a Kentucky native, now

makes his contribution; "You can find reasons all you like," he says, "I think they fought because they were told to fight."

"Maybe," the teacher explains, "but until you have some more evidence than your opinion, we'll go along with what Harriet said."

"Now," the teacher continues, "when we discuss Reconstruction and the years following, we'll find this same argument of white supremacy used to justify and defend . . . what? anybody know?"

And a boy quietly says "Segregation."[12]

Role-playing again, moving from the specific detail to the generalization, the topic of white supremacy and segregation at a time when Birmingham, Selma, and Mississippi were making headlines, the clash of opinions—all suggest that these components of curriculum materials shape and breathe life into a teaching strategy.

STAGES FOR ONE STRATEGY

If a teaching strategy, like curriculum material, is a tool, then toward what ends should it be used? The answer is brief: The aims of the curriculum spelled out in the last chapter are the proper aims of instruction. How the teaching strategy is to be used and developed over a period of time, however, is a more knotty issue and demands explanation.

Initially, a teaching strategy employing the components I've suggested must connect up with youngsters. Pre-schoolers and early primary children bring to school a strong desire to learn. But something happens in school. Making contact with

12. Martin Mayer, *Social Studies in American Schools* (Harper and Row, 1963), pp. 158–160.

children or motivating them to learn develops into a major problem as they mature. Extrinsic forms of motivation—competition, fear, gaining teacher's approval—help, but over the long haul provide little payoff. In the upper grades, disinterest, apathy, putting teachers on, docility, or outright hostility characterize too many youths. Most, however, have learned to endure. Thus, connecting up with kids is absolutely critical. It is the first step of a three-part strategy.

But grabbing them is no easy matter. The three phases of this teaching strategy in the hands of an individual who has gained the respect of the youngsters will play to their strengths and combined with creative instructional materials will maximize (but not guarantee) the possibility that a connection will be made. It means hard work.

Achieving contact may take a month, two, perhaps a semester, or it may never happen at all. Evidences of contact are youngsters willing to speak to you before, during, and after class and school; the satisfying tingle you feel after a particularly volatile discussion where students, especially the "inarticulate" ones, open up and express themselves candidly, drawing from their experiences; kids asking you "why" questions; rising student output in assignments and extra-credits; a relaxed, friendly climate in a classroom. Yet, paradoxically, if the connection is made, the really tough job has only just begun.

Too many capable teachers pride themselves on grabbing kids, "turning them on" is the current phrase, and then dust off their hands in satisfaction when the task has been completed. On the contrary, making contact with students means that they are ready to learn, not that they have learned; it is the take-off point. In the gush of enthusiasm over successfully triggering discussions with low-income children, some bright teachers stop to catch their breath and congratulate themselves, then proceed no further. Unintentionally, they have established a low ceiling on intellectual performance, in effect treating poor children in a perversely condescending way.

The second stage in the development of the teaching strategy is the systematic teaching of skills and knowledge. As I indicated in the last chapter, top priority should be given to the improvement and refinement of academic, intellectual, and interpersonal skills. Perhaps an additional word on skill development may fill in some gaps.

By skills, I mean reading, writing, listening, speaking, thinking, computing, and interpersonal skills required of children in order for them to perform at an effective level once formal education ends. Within each category of skills, there are clusters of sub-skills requiring different levels of sophistication. In reading, for example, there is the difference between word-attack (Herbert Kohl on *psyche*) and verbal skills (see "Bull-jive"). In group work, as described in some of the selections, learning to deal with others in task situations incorporates a broad range of interpersonal skills. Benjamin Bloom and his associates ranked and explained intellectual and affective skills in their *Taxonomy of Educational Objectives: Cognitive and Affective Domains.* While it makes for difficult reading, once understood, the specific skills Bloom describes become valid teaching objectives.

As many others have pointed out, these skills should be generative, capable of being applied to other situations. Some are terminal—cabinet-making, printing, shoemaking; others are generative—problem-solving, techniques of inquiry, handling one's self in a group and understanding the dynamics of that group. The priority, in my opinion, should be equipping children with the generative skills, using areas of knowledge agreed upon by teachers as the vehicles to teach those mental operations. Yes, I want poor kids to be creative; yes, I want poor kids to know about Shakespeare (but not for western culture's sake), to paint like Picasso, and to sing like the Supremes. But most important, I want them to be able to compete on equal terms with the best trained child coming out of expensive private schools. Plush private schools are not my model of excellence; yet to want less cheats inner-city children and, what is worse, sacrifices them on the altar of white middle-class liberals' and black activists' elitist visions of a better world.

How, then, to teach these skills. So far, I have stressed that the physical learning style is closely associated with inductive learning—that is, proceeding from the specific to the general, emphasizing the child's inquiring and learning.

Let me deal briefly with inductive and deductive teaching. The deductive teaching strategy, where exposition looms large, where one proceeds from the abstract to the specific, and where the bulk of intellectual activity originates and ends with the teacher's explanations, clarifications, and demonstrations of proof, is most familiar to teachers since that is the way they have been taught (but not necessarily the way they have learned). It appears as an opposite to the inductive approach.

As translated into materials and techniques, the inductive approach stresses the process of drawing tentative conclusions from evidence. In terms of materials, induction can range from purist—e.g., all evidence, few clues, little direction from the teacher—to highly structured lessons that take students by the mind and lead them from fact to conclusion—e.g., as in programed materials.

In terms of techniques, teachers try to question with more precision, depend upon greater student involvement and interaction. The idealized model of the inductive classroom is one in which students are busily doing things individually and in small groups, suggesting hypotheses, checking them out against available evidence, and "discovering" concepts that can be applied elsewhere. The teacher develops the framework of a learning situation and acts as a stimulator and resource person who works with individual students and groups. Nondirective, the ideal inductive teacher joins students in the search for truth. Of course, it is a far cry from the idealized model to what acutally transpires in classrooms. In the past decade, inductive learning has caught on (although the academic backlash threatens continually) in government-sponsored curriculum reform efforts. These projects, along with what has filtered down into the classrooms (and even penetrated Academe), run the gamut of techniques and materials mentioned above. There is simply no one inductive approach. At best, it is a mixed bag.

And none of the hoopla about induction is new. Many teachers have intuitively used these techniques, from Socrates to the Harvard professor, Louis Agassiz, who once threw out a bunch of old bones to a student and asked him to "see what (he) could make of them" to a teacher in a one-room school house encouraging a group of odd-aged students to continue puttering around an old auto-engine to figure out the principle of internal combustion. The National Science Foundation, Jerome Bruner's writings, and the impetus from Jerrold Zachaiarias's Educational Services, Inc. (now EDC, Education Development Center), an organization that mobilized scholars and teachers in a unique venture in the early 60's to produce curricula materials, sparked much of the new Deweyism and current curricular reform underway in the nation. (Incidentally, one of the early ESI lessons was for youngsters to put together a box of bones.)

Much of the ferment has yet to penetrate inner-city schools. Where it has, teachers unaccustomed to the rationale and spirit behind the material doggedly ask kids to copy, recite, and memorize concepts instead of facts. Students in my homeroom last year were painstakingly copying the nitrogen cycle from a diagram in a new inductive biology text. Because teachers were not asking the four basic questions of curriculum materials and since they were not trained to use these materials, they handled them as they would any other lesson and unit placed before them. Acceptance of inductive materials and techniques is slowed by foot-dragging administrators who shy away from inconvenient changes but, more specifically, by teachers who are unfamiliar and insecure with materials that require modifications of the deductive approaches they are most comfortable with. That inductive approaches may involve a sharing of power between teacher and students only stiffens the resistance.

A number of curriculum reform projects have awakened to this reality and allocate a significant amount of their budget to training teachers to use their materials. Robert Davis of the Madison Math Project filmed lessons, hired sharp teachers and, with suitcases full of materials, trained teachers to use inductive techniques by having inner-city teachers themselves go through the step-by-step operations that kids would perform. EDC follows the same course with their science materials. Still, much more needs to be done in getting teachers to adopt an inductive approach.

Although the inductive approach is congenial to inner-city children, I do not urge that all teachers of the poor adopt "discovery" learning as *the* method. There are problems connected with it.

1. Everything there is to know or do does not have to be discovered by kids. Some information and concepts can be effectively taught in a deductive manner.

2. Whoever prepares materials for children controls what is to be discovered; at best, it can be crude manipulation and, at worst, it often degenerates into a guessing game—i.e., the concept to be learned becomes more important than the process of inquiring.

3. Too often a few articulate kids do the discovering, make all the eureka noises, and the majority of students remain uninvolved. Teachers, carried away because they have structured a lesson so well, reward the few with praise. If discovery is its own reward, what about those who do not participate?

4. There is little provision in the inductive approach for practice and consolidation of what is learned. Because something is discovered does not mean it is learned forever. Any teacher will tell you that some kids (like most adults) discover the same thing over and over again. Practice is critical.

5. Low-income kids accustomed to the deductive style of teaching hesitate to commit themselves to a conclusion based upon their findings. They have been told so often that they must listen to the teacher that they distrust their judgment. Dependency doesn't nurture inquiry. Clearly, this is less a defect of induction and more a slap at how kids have been

taught. Still, an awareness of how they have been taught to learn should inform any effort to alter traditional instruction.

For these reasons, I would suggest a mixed teaching strategy employing the four components mentioned earlier combined with a mixture of exposition and inquiry, always remembering that the process is more important than the piece of knowledge learned. Deductive techniques and materials have their place in the inner-city school, but only insofar as they support skill development.

The lack of practice and consolidation inherent in inductive instruction brings me to the third and last stage in a teaching strategy for inner-city children. Making contact with youngsters and teaching skills through highly interesting content make the third stage—consolidation—critical. David Ausubel hit this point when he wrote:

> By insisting on consolidation or mastery of ongoing lessons before new material is introduced, we make sure of continued readiness and success in sequentially organized learning. Abundant experimental research has confirmed the proposition that prior learnings are not transferable to new learning tasks unless they are first overlearned. Overlearning, in turn, requires an adequate number of . . . spaced repetitions and reviews . . . and opportunity for differential practice of the more difficult components of a task. . . .[13]

I'm not arguing for mindless drill and rote memory; I am emphasizing that structured and sequential materials should include exercises that ask students to apply what they have learned; summaries interspersed liberally throughout re-

13. David P. Ausubel, "A Teaching Strategy for Culturally Deprived Pupils," in Staten Webster (ed.), *Educating the Disadvantaged Learner,* (Chandler, 1966), p. 469.

quiring use of the knowledge they have been exposed to. It is the repeated use of these skill operations that achieve what Ausubel calls "over-learning."

Without such exercises, summaries, quizzes, tests, and the like, curriculum materials and instruction may tap interests and generate sporadic enthusiasm but little more than that. Physical skills call for constant practice; mental skills need no less.

Thus far, I have dealt with the teacher as an instructional decision-maker and developer of curriculum materials. Strategies for each have been suggested and examples have been given. The third facet of the teacher's role is his involvement in the community.

Chapter VI

The Teacher and the Community

Brooklyn, N.Y. May 26—On Herkimer Street, outside Junior High School 271 one day last week, there must have been 150 policemen, guarding an almost empty school.

It was 2:45 P.M. and some teachers were beginning to straggle home from the big, low-slung red-brick building. Elaine Rooke, PTA president, member of the local governing board of the Ocean-Hill-Brownsville Experimental School District . . . watched scornfully.

"See that," she demanded. "I'm glad the press is here to see that. It's not even 3 and already they're going home. They do that every day."

The children—there are 9,000 of them (mostly black

> and Puerto-Rican) in eight schools in the district—have been in and out of the buildings so often in the last two weeks that it will be a feat, when this is over, to calculate the amount of attendance-based state funds that the district will lose.
>
> On this particular day, there had been only a handful of kids where usually JHS 271 was thick with kids, some 2000 of them. Today they were home, or in "freedom schools" set up by the governing board when it decided to boycott all eight schools.
>
> The governing board voted on May 7 to order the transfer out of the district of 13 teachers and six supervisors, whom it accused of trying to disrupt the decentralization experiment. They refused to go, claiming the action amounted to arbitrary dismissal without due process and as such was illegal. They received the immediate backing of their . . . union. . . .
>
> When they tried to return, the day after they received the notices, the five who had been ousted at 271 were blocked at the door by a mixture of parents, community people and sympathizers. . . . JHS 271 was now the focus and the symbol of the controversy. . . .[1]

Waves of protest and change dash against the schoolhouse door. Decentralization, community schools, experimental programs, boycotts, freedom schools—all testify to the buffeting that teachers and administrators have received over the past few years. Indignantly, they ask: To whom do the schools belong? And the question just as indignantly, is hurled back: Yes, to *whom* do the schools belong?

Although the issues of control and power have recently emerged in low-income areas, voicelessness and lack of partici-

1. *Washington Post,* May 27, 1968, p. 6.

pation sum up the inner-city community's traditional role in the affairs of the school. Unsurprisingly, relationships between the poor and their schools have been hostile and abrasive.

Perceptions help to explain such imperfect relationships. Inside the school, too many teachers and principals see the community and its inhabitants as deprived and depraved. Try these quotes from a favorable article praising the efforts of the Teacher Corps in Memphis, Tennessee.

> BLACKBOARD REFLECTS HOMES BARE OF CULTURE AND BOOKS
>
> "Dis." The letters written in chalk by a Negro boy stand out with brutal reality on the blackboard.
>
> "I tell them that they should say "this," not "dis," Mrs. Peggy Pickles said wearily. "But I don't believe I reach very many."
>
> She realizes that when the children leave her classroom . . . they return to homes steeped in cultural and economic poverty.
>
> In many of the homes there are no books. The spoken language is a dialect of limited vocabulary. Before coming to school the children may not have known that the written word existed.
>
> "They don't care about school. They don't know that educational skills can give them the opportunity to be successful. Yes, I'm always frustrated. . . ."
>
> "In any poverty area school there are certain factors that affect people," said Dr. Jack Miller, the director of the Mid-South Teacher Corps. . . . "The children are not competitive. They lack aspirations and the desire or drive to do well. This begins to affect the teachers."[2]

2. Memphis (Tenn.) *Commercial Appeal,* January 15, 1968, p. 8.

Blame the Jews, not the Nazis; blame the victim, not the murderer. But such logic about kids and parents is not unusual. Remember the principal's letter of orientation to his teachers in Chapter 1. Chock full of condescension, it pictured a community of parents unconcerned with their children and deprived of the "cultural" background necessary for success in school. The attitudes of Mr. Brown and Mrs. Smith toward kids and community were expressed in Chapter 2. They are familiar to any teacher who has spent time in school lounges and boiler rooms.

Yet teachers or principals who have taken the time to meet and speak with parents must know that poor parents have high aspirations (sociologists would remind us, however, that these are unrealistic) and a steady—albeit eroding—faith in the dollars and mobility that public education promises.

Parents want their children to learn how to read, write, and compute. They want their kids to make it. In Washington, D.C., a few years ago, a large sample of low-income families was exhaustively studied. In two publications, parents spoke of education.

> My husband didn't have no education and had to do laboring work. If my children could read, they could get a job driving a truck or working in a store. They could learn to use the cash register if they know how to add. They can be somebody. If you don't have no education, you have to take the first thing they give you. If you go to an employment agency, you'd get a job probably dishwashing since you had no education. I want them to do something better.
>
> The time is soon coming when you will need a college degree to sweep the street.

> Gloria and Peter were slow readers and I helped them learn to read better and develop a vocabulary. . . . I called the teacher last week and asked her how he was doing. I also helped Sue develop a vocabulary. Now she is secretary for one of the school clubs. . . . Gloria . . . is trying real hard to do well in school. She now has large black circles under her eyes and the doctor . . . says she will have to have glasses. Welfare is giving glasses soon. The truant officer was here because Gloria had to stay out of school for two weeks due to her eye condition. I was upset when the truant officer came because if there is one thing I do it is to make sure that the children [she has 12] are able to keep their school attendance up. . . . The minute the truant officer came I called up Welfare and was told to bring the slip for the glasses up there. That was the day I went straight up to Welfare with the slip and walked [3½ miles] home because I did not have a car token.[3]

If, skeptics might ask, the poor know the value of education and its rewards, why do they not carry through on their aspirations? The Child Rearing Study of Low Income Families concluded that the poor can't practice what they preach because they "lack the money, the know-how, and the contacts for helping children realize educational goals." If home and school clash, it is not over the value of education. The answer lies elsewhere.

Although poor parents want what all of us want for our children, what they get, sadly, is illiteracy, dropouts, unemployed sons and daughters, and explanations: the home has no books; the family doesn't take kids to the museums; the

3. First two paragraphs, p. 198, from *Poverty's Children,* pp. 20–21. Last paragraph from p. 25 of *Culture, Class and Poverty.* Both publications of CROSSTELL, Health and Welfare Council of the National Capital Area, 1966–1967.

neighborhood isn't conducive to healthy living. While each of these statements has a grain of truth, they have been developed by schoolmen into elaborate alibis for doing little.

Besides selective perceptions, another reason why teachers and administrators deeply believe that their efforts are seriously undercut and outflanked by parent and community is that the school itself teaches teachers to believe it. Orientation workshops, the intellectual climate of the school, and the prevailing opinions of veteran teachers informally and formally instruct even the brightest, well-intentioned neophyte that the school is an isolated bastion of civilization surrounded by natives anxious to eliminate the good done by the school. Estelle Fuchs underscores this process in her description of a new teacher in an inner-city school.

A teacher-training project recorded the impressions of first-year teachers. The following is one excerpt from a first-grade teacher:

> Mrs. Jones, the sixth grade teacher, and I were discussing reading problems. I said, "I wonder about my children. They seem average. Some of them even seem to be above average. I can't understand how they can grow up to be fifth- and sixth graders and still be reading on the second grade level. It seems absolutely amazing."
>
> Mrs. Jones (an experienced teacher) explained about the environmental problems that these children have. "Some of them never see a newspaper. Some of them have never been on the subway. The parents are so busy having parties and things that they have no time for their children. They can't even take them to a museum or anything. It's very important that the teacher stress books."
>
> Mrs. Jones tells her class, "If anyone asks you what you want for Christmas, you can say you want a book." She told

> me that she had a 6-1 class (the top group) last year, and it was absolutely amazing how many children had never seen a newspaper. They can't read Spanish either. So she said that the educational problem lies with the parents. They are the ones that have to be educated. . . .

Fuchs describes how this sensitive, concerned young teacher began to accept the assumptions of her colleagues, especially when asked by the principal, a few months after school started, to divide up her class to distribute among three other classes so that she could teach another group. How did she choose which kids would go where? By the results of the reading readiness tests. Kids were being tracked as early as the first year into "good" classes and "slow" ones. By January, the new teacher had concluded:

> I believe my school is a pretty good school. It isn't in the best neighborhood. . . . *You have to remember that in a school such as ours the children are not ready and willing to learn as in the schools in middle-class neighborhoods* [italics added].[4]

Teachers are apt pupils.

The perceptions of parents, of course, aren't perfect either. There are some teachers and administrators who work with youngsters and parents intensely and sincerely. Nat Hentoff's *Our Children Are Dying* (Viking, 1966) is a testimonial to Elliot Shapiro, a principal in a Harlem school. The evidence is there but it reveals only the outstanding individuals who can muster time and energy beyond that required

4. Estelle Fuchs, "How Teachers Learn to Help Children Fail," *Transaction*, September, 1968, pp. 45–48.

for a full day in the classroom. There are such teachers and administrators but not in sufficient numbers, unfortunately, to alter the rigid views of angry parents.

What we have then, on the one hand, are parents serious about the education of their children and, on the other hand, schoolmen believing that parents and community are hostile to their efforts.

As others have pointed out, the gap between low-income community and school may be due to class differences, color, value conflict, and the like. No doubt such explanations have validity and evidence can be marshaled to support each of them. But none of these explanations attacks one of the deeper problems that has become both a cause and effect of that distance between home and school. That problem is the myth of professionalism.

By myth I mean the belief that schoolmen know precisely how kids must be taught, how they should learn, and their "true" nature. Certainty, not inquiry, defines that belief. In an effort to establish professional identity, teachers and administrators compare themselves to doctors. The analogy of medicine is often flung up as a barrier to prevent concerned parents from questioning procedures, regulations, and policy. Teachers and principals, the dogma runs, know so much more about instruction, curriculum, and scheduling than parents do that to expect intelligent questions and helpful suggestions from them is like asking a cancer patient for his opinion on whether chemotherapy or cobalt treatment should be used on him.

The analogy, of course, is ridiculous. Not that teachers do not have more information at their fingertips about these matters than laymen; indeed, if they didn't, something would be seriously amiss. But information is not wisdom. And any teacher who has maintained his honesty will tell you how much he does not know. The helplessness and frustration of teachers in answering questions about motivation, the learning process, and behavior are well-known to informed observers. Diagnosis and prescription in inner-city schools remain, at best, a seat-of-the-pants operation.

Frantically trying to establish professionalism and to prevent parental interference, educators have let loose a smoke screen of scientific jargon which obscures rather than clarifies issues. Only in the past decade, thanks to the civil rights and black movements, has the smoke screen lifted to reveal schoolmen trying to cover up their professional nakedness by pointing at parents and blaming them for low reading and achievement scores. After blame, guilt follows, with fear not far behind.

If you doubt this, try asking an inner-city principal for his school's reading scores broken down by grade and class during his tenure. If releasing test scores is not school policy, he will probably confess that he doesn't possess such information or suggest you see someone down in research. Perhaps he will just say no. If he is a decent sort, he may explain patiently that reading scores are not an accurate index of learning. He will probably point out to you the transiency of pupils, their impoverished background, and terrible learning handicaps, ending with the observation that his staff is doing a superior job with their students.

If you persist, however, by pointing out that most schools list scholarship winners, finalists in contests, and other honors won by pupils, thereby implying that the school has done a successful job—why not, then, publish reading scores? At this point, if your experience was like mine, explanations cease and the air turns cold.

But if you maintain your poise by agreeing with the principal that such scores are not a valid measure of a school's success yet remain an important benchmark and a rough one at that for parents to assess the school's ability to perform, chances are the conversation is about to end. You are facing a standoff. Unless there is a system-wide policy on informing parents of a school's performance, the principal will usher you out of his office, perhaps, inviting you to step into a classroom where the "noise of learning" will convince you more than statistics will of the school's success.

Such pseudo-professionalism must be confronted and exposed since it is only a sham excuse contrived to insulate educators from the clients they are pledged to serve. "Professionalism" is the code word for keeping poor parents at arm's length.

Because of this myth, no meaningful face-to-face contact between school and parent, between teacher and community can develop. Because schoolmen react negatively to inquiries about the performance of youngsters, teachers, or the school, no personal relationships with the broad spectrum of the community can develop.

Certainly to read some of the professional advice, one would reach this conclusion. Consider what one professor of education advised administrators and teachers to do if they wanted to know about their community. He recommended "Ten Easy Lessons" in four hours—a kind of instant community involvement. They are:

> 1. *Talk to your Board of Education. . . .*
> You'll gain some valuable information regarding the

characteristics, customs and traditions of the community. In turn, the board will be happy to know of your interests in this area of your work. . . .

2. *Confer with the local manager of the Chamber of Commerce or locally prominent businessman. . . .*

These individuals will have had many contacts with the various "publics" of the community. . . .

3. *Arrange to see the mayor or other city official. . . .*

4. *Visit with the president of the local Ministerial Association or any minister in the community. . . .*

The minister's role calls for a close association with the people of a community. His particular role provides him with rather sensitive insights into the community relations. . . .

5. *Arrange to visit with the editor(s) of the local newspaper. . . .*

6. *Ask your secretary to arrange a 30 minute conference with your chief administrative assistants. . . .*

7. *Arrange to have morning coffee with one or more of the presidents of the local civic clubs. . . .*

The Rotary, Lions or Kiwanis Club presidents are in daily contact with people in the community. . . .

8. *Ask the local PTA Council for 30 minutes at their next planning meeting. . . .*

9. *Decide upon a teacher group with which you will visit about community relationships. . . .*

10. *While other publics, groups, agencies, and/or individuals in the community* perhaps should be contacted, you already have enough information to provide valuable help in your work as a new community and educational leader (sic).[5]

Indeed, "a new community and educational leader." What garbage! Is it any wonder that critics accuse the school system

5. M. Scott Norton, "Know Your Community in Ten Easy Lessons," *Clearing House*, September, 1968, pp. 55–57.

of maintaining the status quo? The community that teachers and administrators who follow these ten steps would come to know is middle- and upper-class white. Dominant in business and political affairs, this slice of the community becomes *the* community to schoolmen thereby excluding the ethnic poor of both races. Thus, the current unrest in inner-city communities emerges from two sources inextricably intertwined. One source is the dissatisfaction of a militant minority and a silent majority with the quality of education. Their children have been ignored. The other source is the drive for more political influence and power by previously excluded groups. Both are so intertwined that it is difficult to sort them. But both must be recognized and dealt with.[6]

If creating more mechanisms that involve low-income parents and the community meaningfully in decision-making is necessary to deal with one of these sources of discontent, another means of dealing with the other source is using teachers as the instrument for humanizing relationships between school and community.

6. Defining "community" causes more problems than it resolves. Try, for instance, to pick a group that represents an inner-city community. Who gets on it? The loudest militant? Representatives of the NAACP? SNCC? Black Panthers? Urban League? Ministers Alliance? Businessmens' association? A welfare mother? Director of the local anti-poverty center? Elections run the same risk of reflecting an unrepresentative slice of the community.

Obviously the "community" is diverse and that diversity should be mirrored in elected and appointed positions. What happens, unfortunately, is that the shrillest may end up representing the community. In some instances there are gatekeepers, mostly white and middle-class, who often listen to what they want to hear, and the community they perceive may, in fact, exist only in their fantasy.

HUMANIZING SCHOOLS

This lack of humaneness, of meaningful relationships between community and school, is the root cause of existing raw feelings between the two. If teachers and administrators knew parents and were familiar with the dynamics and rhythm of life in the community, assuming that they were effective in the classroom, slogans about decentralization, local control, and community schools would generate less heat. It is possible to avoid the Biafra of bitterness that befell the 1968 New York City conflict over local control and the effect it has had on other school systems. School and community can mesh gears and work together without the corrosive confrontation of black and white, parent and teacher, on opposite sides of the barricades. New York is a preview of coming attractions unless school systems can react imaginatively. Now whether the schools are capable of an imaginative reaction is, unfortunately, another and more difficult question.

More face-to-face contacts between school staff and community over issues involving school children could bring a humaneness to community relations that is so obviously missing. Bringing community people into the school as paid aides is one step. Another is hiring community workers as part of the faculty. Joint planning between community leaders and schoolmen is another possibility. None of these, however, deal with the larger issue of broadening the vision of teachers to enable them to see their role and function as being actively involved with parents and participating in community life as an extension of their interest in kids. Unless that is done, pre-professionals and community coordinators will merely generate more intra-school squabbling.

Infiltrating the school with community people probably won't make teachers more aware of their broader role, nor will teachers' unions. Perhaps at one time the slogan used in the 1967 New York teachers walk-out—"Teachers Want What Children Need"—may have been valid, but no longer. Ocean Hill-Brownsville in 1968–1969 pitted parents against teachers and erased what once appeared to be a natural alliance.

As teacher unionization proceeds, the traditional interests of trade unionism (and I include the NEA also) will prevail even at the risk of alienating poor parents. To look to unions to deliver the humaneness and involvement that I call for must await the time when unions nail down the higher salaries and security they have pledged to their membership. I doubt that unions can now place high on their agenda the humanizing of school services.

Whether school boards and administrators can muster the will to change the role of the teacher is also debatable. What is not debatable, however, is the necessity for teachers to get out of their fortresses and into the neighborhoods. They must work with youngsters in non-authoritarian settings. They must get to know people in the community. These things must be done, if for no other reason (and there are others) than to improve the quality of instruction.

Simply stated, effective teaching is intimately related to how well a teacher knows who his charges are and the nature of their surroundings. If he doesn't, his perceptions will continue to be shaped by TV, newspapers, social science formulas, and fear—not by first-hand experience. And by experience I don't mean bus tours through the slums, hurried walks up and down streets, or unannounced welfare-like visits. No instant urban sociology. I mean the tough business of getting to know people who live in the area.

Let the community teach the teacher. In New York, for example, a group called *Teachers, Inc.,* organized and operated by teachers, contracted to train people for the classroom. They had the trainees live in the community during the summer, used neighborhood and university resources to help trainees to see the community as a school itself in which much can be learned and used in the formal classroom. In doing so, they got to know people in the community well.

These relationships more than any sociological profile will create that base of information from which a teacher can make essential instructional and curricular decisions. More important is what facts can do to perceptions. Except for the bigot, getting to know the community through individuals would permit teachers to sort out assumptions and attitudes about the poor and test them against flesh-and-blood evidence. No abstract theorizing. To some, initial beliefs may be confirmed. Face-to-face contact might produce a negative reaction. My hunch, however, is that most educators, given a comprehensive and supervised experience in the community and then set loose, will see the poor as they are: a diverse group of human beings who have learned to survive on a marginal income. I don't think teachers, black or white, who profess interest in working with the "disadvantaged" can understand this unless they can sit down comfortably and have a beer with a man who is trying to raise five kids on the wages of a short-order cook. For "professional" reasons, then, it is imperative that teachers re-examine fundamental assumptions about the poor, assumptions that have been proved to

influence the achievement of children—re-examine them through individual contacts.
Presently, about 90 percent of a teacher's time is spent in
Where division begins is on the answers to such questions as:

- When are already overburdened teachers going to do all this community work?
- What specifically should teachers do?
- Do the roles of teacher and community worker conflict?

As things stand now, the teacher doesn't have the time. Presently, about 90 percent of a teacher's time is spent in telling, clarifying, and summarizing information for small and large groups of students. In most public schools there are anywhere from 25 to 30 contact periods a week with at least five and in some cases up to seven occurring each day, to say nothing of the collecting, record-keeping, and myriad non-teaching chores. Visit some schools between two and three o'clock if you want a picture of exhausted teachers and exhausted kids clock-watching.

If the instructional load is reduced, say, to one-third or one-half of what it is now, then teachers would have the time to wear three very different but extremely important hats: instructor, curriculum developer, and liaison agent with the community.

The role of the teacher, as has been suggested throughout this book, must change. To make the change staff must be increased by at least a third. And that, of course, means more money. To the anguished cries of taxpayers one can only ask what is more practical: To continue pouring down the drain millions of dollars to train teachers when everyone knows that within a decade only a handful of those trained will still be in the classrooms, or to invest funds to restructure the conventional role of the teacher in order to make classroom teaching an attractive career and thus retain teachers? While the mandate seems clear, what government or foundation researchers have the guts to measure the cost effectiveness of current teacher education against the potential returns of reshaping career positions?

These questions aside, the fact remains that most teachers even if they had the inclination simply don't have the emotional and physical resources or time to get involved. Thus, allotment of time for this facet of teaching is crucial. Were I suggesting something radical or unheard of, I might tiptoe through sentences with cautious qualifiers, but the fact is that community involvement as part of a tripartite teaching role has been and continues to be emphasized in various parts of the country.

A number of programs have implemented this concept. Across the country, the Teacher Corps has spread community involvement into over one-hundred school systems in thirty states. In Washington, D.C., the Urban Teacher Corps (the Cardozo Project in Urban Teaching described earlier) has trained intern teachers for seven years.

Even against this slow penetration, schoolmen raise predictable objections. They agree that the tripartite teaching role is both viable and necessary but because it requires a sizable and costly increase in staff, the concept is "unrealistic." The cheap way, of course, and the direction usually taken, is to hire community coordinators or "indigenous" aides. Both are useful but ineffective in ultimately altering the hostile relationships that have grown up between school and community.

The recent determined thrusts by poor people in major

cities to gain control of their schools is another way of altering existing arrangements. That each effort is laden with pitfalls and is not a magical formula should be self-evident. I wonder if wiser heads have fully explored the potential payoff involved in changing the conventional role of the teacher both in terms of its educational value and in rebuilding the shattered confidence of the community in the schools.

TEACHERS IN THE COMMUNITY

What are some of the activities that teachers engage in, provided they have the time and training? Again the available guidelines come from scattered programs such as the ones mentioned. Perhaps a few examples of what some teachers have done would give a more specific picture of what I am referring to.

The following excerpts come from reports submitted to me when I directed the Cardozo Project in Urban Teaching from 1965–1967. Intern teachers had been introduced to the neighborhoods of the three schools where we were then located by spending one afternoon a week for three months in neighborhood centers of the local anti-poverty program. Remember that the teachers were also teaching a half day in addition to two afternoon graduate seminars at the high school. A Staff member at each neighborhood center was responsible for orienting the teachers to the activities and services of the center besides filling them in on the anatomy of the community. The employment picture, social services, and community organization became familiar to the teachers. Thus, each teacher developed a fund of information that ultimately proved useful in making referrals and suggestions to parents. Obviously, the neighborhood center also benefited since these teachers became their arm in the three local schools. After three months, the teachers were sprung loose to develop some community involvement of their own choice. Individually or in teams, the teachers spent the rest of the school year and the following summer working with people in the community.

Performance was uneven. Besides all the difficulties encountered in beginning a plan without guidelines to follow, there were problems of personality, attitudes, and purpose. I discovered, for example, that those teachers who were having a rough time with their classes were reticent about contacting students or families. When classroom success increased, the desire to meet with students outside class rose correspondingly. Also some teachers felt most strongly that visits with students and their families smacked of social work and this, they felt, was to be avoided. Others wanted to make these contacts but simply could not muster the emotional energy or master the skills required to hurdle the barriers of race and class that, in their minds, loomed ominously.

While these reasons may explain why some of the teachers did not immediately plunge into the lives of their students, it does not touch upon the efforts and responses of those who actively and systematically committed themselves to a program of contacts with students and community. Here are some excerpts from their reports:

Elementary: Female, White

I met Gregory's father in the lot behind Florida Avenue Church after work. Mainly I was looking into Gregory's complaint that his brother ran home before him and ate the lunch their father had prepared for them before he went to work. We had to laugh when his brother appeared as he was smaller and Gregory said that the tale wasn't true. Then his father got angry and told Gregory that there would be no more of this. He also asked me if I knew why the boys' names hadn't appeared on the lunch list, for he had signed at the beginning of school. All we could do for this was wait it out and give him an extra lunch whenever there was one. His name and his brother's are now on the lunch list.

Renaldo and his mother had not come to receive his report card, and as she was at home and not working, I went to see her with her son. Their apartment although in a run down looking building was furnished well, with separate beds for each child, and was clean and warm. The mother has three small children, and as such couldn't come to school. We talked about Renaldo's marks which included a few "no progresses" and the rest "some progresses." The mother was very upset about the minuses in self-control and independence and cooperation. She said that because Renaldo was almost nine years old they would try talking to him about things that needed improvement but that if this didn't work she would have to turn to a spanking, and she told him that she would give him one after school for the disobedience he had been showing. Renaldo accepted this seriously, not as something that was handed out daily, which is not the case with other children's parents I visited. He then read for his mother and I showed her how to help him sound out words or get them by other clues. She reads well and wants definite direction in working with this at home. As none of the school books can be taken home I have been borrowing some from the library and letting some children use them. But I need to check up on the bookmobile service as I don't know of a library close to the homes of most of my children, in fact I know there isn't one.

In the meantime I took two books out of the Mount

Pleasant Branch for Renaldo, and will have him take them home as a beginning book report to work on. He definitely needs to do all the reading he can, and it's great that he's got definite help at home, and a family that is interested in what he's doing.

High School: Female, White

Mary is one of my eleventh grade students with very low reading ability. After noticing the great trouble she was having with reading and any written work, I spoke to her after school. The next day I went with her to see the counselor. He arranged her program to include a reading class second period. This "extra attention" seems to have helped her to be more interested in the class. Her attendance has improved.

Sylvia is a twenty year old eleventh grade student. She is married and has a baby. We have become quite friendly after a few long talks. She is having internal troubles and has been going to the clinic regularly. The doctor is suggesting a serious operation which will make her unable to have children. She does not seem to understand the trouble completely nor is she aware of the alternatives. I spoke with her before her last visit, encouraging her to bring her husband again to the clinic and get all the information possible.

Sylvia is constantly asking me for extra work. I have given her a long term assignment on children's literature. She will be analyzing children's books and learning (from a text on Children's Literature of mine) the importance of reading for children.

She is also interested in part-time work. I suggested that she fill out an application from Mr. Gray. She tried to get a job here at the project office, but her typing is not yet good enough. I suggested she go to the large department stores (in person rather than phoning) to inquire about "Christmas rush" jobs.

I have met three times with my eleventh grade girls. They have decided that our discussion group can do a variety of things. Therefore, they would like it to be a "club." The girls are now thinking of a name for the group.

We meet at Roger's apartment after school. I have found that this informal setting (drinking cokes, sitting on the floor) is a great aid in helping the girls to speak more freely. We have discussed sex at some length. From these talks, I am now more aware of their fear of sex, their sense of shame, and their curiosity. I hope to bring in a speaker to discuss birth control with the group. This is the area in which the girls show the most interest and naïveté. Although eager to talk about the subject, none of the girls connect birth control with their lives, present or future!

We have also discussed "boy-girl" problems and social life at Cardozo. I was interested to learn that social life for these girls does not revolve around school. The boys they date are from their neighborhood or church group. They feel the social life at Cardozo is greatly lacking and the boys are immature.

High School: Male, White

Took student to "walk through" application forms and red tape at public library central office. National Youth Corps student felt overwhelmed by bureaucracy. Asked me to drive him down to office and help him fill out forms. Only took three hours.

Work with consumer education office of NDC #3. Planned section of unit with civics class on "where to shop—how to shop?" Planning field trip and class visit for lecture.

Working with Neighborhood Legal Service to prepare material for unit on criminal law. Planning to coordinate material with Law Reform and Education unit. Also had speaker, young lawyer, talk to Aide class about credit law. Also explained Neighborhood Legal Service to student.

Officer from No. 13 visited class. Students were well prepared with questions based on personal "brushes" with law.

Criticized No. 10 community relations. Police Officer visibly upset. After bell, students surrounded visitor with many questions. Asked him to return. Officer replied he would enjoy making return visit.

Junior High: Female, White

I had two of my ninth grade girls over to the apartment to work on the writing of their autobiographies (which they are doing in class). We worked on writing and rewriting and then talked about Helen Keller, and various careers. One of the girls is interested in being a teacher's aide and the other has no idea what she likes and seems to dislike just about everything except being a housewife and having ten kids. Since these girls will turn sixteen early in '67, I plan to round up some career type information that will suit their abilities. The girl who wants to be the housewife was fascinated with some excerpts from *Children of Sanchez* I used in class. She has borrowed the book and is now doing some independent reading. . . .

High School: Male, White

Recently, a teacher from a neighboring suburban school, called the office to inquire into the possibilities of doing some sort of combined class in History. We felt that our aim was to have students communicate on a level of understanding that they are not able to do as adults because of many deeply rooted feelings. In short, as these students worded it, "We want to learn more about each other."

In the early stages, four of my students and four from James Monroe met for some planning sessions. We went to their school to observe other history classes, and also for the discussion about what we were going to do together. At first, the air was thick with tension, but it soon dissipated into profound discussion about the project's possibilities. As was stated, the kids set as their theme, "To Learn More About Each Other," which we think is a good one.

After two of these such sessions, we agreed that a subtle approach to Civil Rights would be of interest to both schools. It was felt that many of the white students would be expecting a discussion of Civil Rights and would automatically reject it. Instead, we chose to take an historical approach, and really get to the root of the problem, beginning with a unit on slavery.

The slavery unit would last approximately two weeks, and we could meet twice; one time at Cardozo, and one time at Monroe. The students, particularly those from Cardozo, felt that the first session should be held here at Cardozo, since "The Negroes are always coming to the whites with their problems, and it might be better for the whites to feel a bit of the responsibility and obligation, by finding themselves in a minority situation." The conclusion of the unit on slavery would be made at Monroe with both classes meeting together to summarize what had been discussed in the unit, or what had been learned in the unit.

The most interesting lesson for me came when we were returning home from school in my car, and one of my students mentioned what a surprise it was to her, "To find that teachers were human." It was also mentioned how little we knew about each other, and I confess that this was true for me.

Elementary: Female, Black

I visited the home of Jacqueline where she lives with her parents and seven brothers and sisters. I went there early in the afternoon, and found her mother washing with a wringer washer in the kitchen. One of the boys was on the dilapidated couch in the living room, covered with a blanket. He was unable to attend school that day because he had torn his pants, and his mother had misplaced her needle. There was a pre-school age child present, and a baby of a neighbor, whom the mother watched during the day.

The mother was pleased that I visited her, and explained that she never went out because she was nervous. The house was a two-story frame row house and was crumbling with decay. There were clothes lying about in every room. It was a cool day, but the small kerosene stove warmed the living room. She explained that she had been living there four years and her only complaint was its lack of closets.

I spoke to her about Jacqueline, who is an attractive and responsive child. She was pleased and said that she wished that all of her children would always be so. She said, however, that she was worried because her 14-year-old son had been missing for three weeks, and that neither the police nor school officials could find him. She seemed, though uneducated, to be intelligent in her conversation about her children and her hopes for them. The visit ended pleasantly as we talked about the latest episode of one TV soap opera. I told her that if I could be of assistance to her to let me know through Jacqueline.

Elementary: Male, White

Charlie K. was the boy I did my case study on during the summer. Last time in my report I had said that Charlie had cut class and that his mother beat him and attendance had been rather regular. Then one day he and two other boys, one by the name of Gregory who is also in my class, cut school and roamed the halls. A teacher reported them and took them to a counselor. The next day Gregory came to school with some money he had taken from the counselor's desk when she had left the office. He implicated Charlie in the theft. Charlie confessed and returned the money. The counselor said she was going to call in the police, but she never showed up. Everyone was very disappointed in Charlie.

Charlie's punishment in the class was after-school detention. One day after his punishment I took Charlie in my car to Howard University. We went to the gym and watched the athletics. We were there until about 5 P.M. Then I said I had to go home to see my wife and eat. Charlie said he didn't want to go home just yet. He wanted to go to Gregory's house and play. He said he didn't eat dinner until 9:00

P.M. most of the time. Charlie's father ran out on his mother and he doesn't have any new shoes. They probably don't have regular meals at his house.

The only comment Charlie made about what we had seen was to ask "What's the name of that place we were just at?"

High School: Female, White

Another teacher made me aware early in January that one of my students had dropped out of school because she was pregnant. He arranged for me to accompany the girl, Alice, to the Maternity Clinic, 65 Massachusetts Avenue to obtain a verification of pregnancy so that we could proceed to try to get her admitted to Webster School for Girls. When I called Alice, who was a quiet student whom I didn't know very well, but who had done good work for me, she seemed very willing and glad to have me go along with her.

I picked her up at her house and at that time met her father and four or five of her younger brothers and sisters. She's the oldest. Her father is a pleasant, talkative, easy-going man who drives a truck for a construction company. The family had moved to Washington seven or eight years ago from North Carolina and have lived above a store ever since. The mother, whom I later met, works six nights a week as a waitress. She was small, quiet, and seemed uneasy and suspicious of me. They did not talk about the pregnancy and I gathered that Alice had tried for quite some time to conceal it from them. The home was clean and neat, but in very poor condition. There were two TV sets and a new car.

The clinic is housed in an old, dingy school building. The maternity clinic itself consists of two medium-sized rooms with makeshift offices surrounding each. The first is for incoming patients, mostly young Negro girls. We gave our names and waited 45 minutes, while Alice got more and more jittery. She kept making comments about all the sloppy-looking "nurses" or technicians we saw moving about and joking with each other. She said she didn't think they looked like nurses and she didn't want any of them touching her. We talked about her husband (she had gotten married a couple of days before), whom she had known for two years and had planned to marry when they finished school. He had just gotten a job and dropped out of school and was living with her family for the time being. He is a Cardozo student since September when he came up from North Carolina to live with an aunt and uncle. Alice said at this point she thought the baby was due in about June. She also talked about how she wished she could get rid of it and how her mother was going to call "some man" who could do it.

We were called into the reception office and the woman immediately demanded to know why Alice's mother wasn't with her and who I was. She assumed that Alice was not married and told her her mother had to be along for the doctor to examine her. We explained that she was married and were told she had to have her marriage license with her (true for girls 16 and under).

We were given an appointment for the next day and when we asked about Webster School, we were referred to a social worker who, after another wait, admitted us and again wanted to know who I was and why I was so interested. As we had been waiting in the second waiting room to see her, we saw the doctor's office at one end of the room and the patient's dressing room at the other end. The door to the examination room kept opening so that everyone in the waiting room could see the patient inside. The girls had to change into a hospital gown in the dressing room and then walk through the waiting room and sometimes sit down and wait again before going in to be examined. Alice got more nervous again, and was very quiet, and uneasy when we got in to see Mrs.—, the social worker. Mrs.— kept talking to me about Alice as if Alice weren't there and when she did address Alice it was in a sugary tone: "May I ask . . .?" She explained that she would have to wait for verification of pregnancy, but would take down information now and send the forms to Webster after the doctor's examination.

Alice took me up immediately on my offer to come back with her the second day. On our way out the first day, we stopped at the Birth Control Clinic. They gave us pamphlets but said they could do no more unless the client had at least one living child, even though she was married.

The next day we waited 1 hour and 15 minutes after our scheduled appointment time. We then talked to another lady, who again made a big fuss over who I was and why I was there. She was to interview Alice on her financial situation to see if she qualified for aid. First she examined the marriage license and discovered that Alice had falsified her age and her husband his since they didn't have his parents' consent for the marriage. Alice said her parents told her to do it so they could get married. The woman decided to overlook it after telling Alice she didn't think it was a very good idea. After asking several questions she determined that since Alice said her husband was making $70/week he was above the maximum ($200/month) to receive assistance. So she explained the costs of hospitalization at the various hospitals and told Alice where she could get free pre-natal care (clinic at 14th and Q). I got information about what she should do if she was mistaken about the amount her husband was making or if his income dropped, and we were given instructions to go to 817–9th Street, N.W.

I had to leave before Alice was examined. She was very nervous but when I called her later she said it had gone all right. She had been told the baby seemed healthy, she was given vitamin pills and a diet and an appointment for later in the month at the clinic.

After going through the school nurse, and calling Alice several times trying to get her to call Webster herself, I gave up on getting her in especially since the baby was due so early. I worked instead on trying to help her husband get enrolled at Cardozo Night School since he said he wanted to finish school. His section teacher was very bitter about the boy because he had gone out of his way to help him and had been let down a number of times, and in the end, as the section teacher predicted, he decided not to go to night school.

ASSESSING TEACHERS IN THE COMMUNITY

How nice it would have been to record success stories, happy endings, and startling results. There were a few but only of a minor variety. These teachers were inexperienced, forced to play their roles by ear, constantly keeping their fingers crossed. But they did get out of the classroom with students and meet parents and neighbors on a face-to-face basis. In doing so, they discovered the diversity of poor people, re-examined many of their basic assumptions about race and class, and, probably, realized the complexity of teaching in inner-city schools. They began to see with more clarity than textbooks or learned lectures could ever convey, the meaning of ghetto life. The process of seeing kids as individuals telescoped so that a name in a class took on a face, parents, friends, and a home. The necessity of making myriad, complex decisions about instruction, curriculum materials, and simple conversational give and take that is so important to youngsters began to take on deeper and fuller meaning. The community is an effective teacher.

Inevitably, frustration and depression set in because teachers saw clearly the tragic deficiencies that exist in the present system of education. Intern teachers made these discoveries much sooner than their more experienced colleagues, who were shackled to an excessive teaching load and burdensome clerical trivia. Overburdened teachers see only faces and bodies move in and out of their rooms; they are insulated and isolated from the lives of their students.

The discoveries that the teachers who are involved in the community make, as depressing as some are, I count as a strength. Slicing through rhetoric and platitudes, teachers realize that while they are capable of making some changes and having some impact, they are limited. Limited by institutional constraints and limited by the point in time when they intervene in a child's life, teachers nevertheless can gain a realistic perspective on inner-city schools that is all too often missing in most of their colleagues and sideline critics.

Living with complexity, an awareness of one's limitations, yet trying to make the most of them, some teachers in this program and Teacher Corps efforts across the country have developed imaginative activities in and out of the classroom.

Newspaper articles, magazine pieces, and TV have spotlighted a few such efforts like store-front study centers, after-school tutorials, organization of father and mother clubs, work with community agencies, and establishment of dropout schools. Once community involvement becomes a fixed and expected function of the classroom teacher, the only ceiling on his activities is his own imagination.

Actually, that is not quite accurate because with community involvement teachers are confronted with the serious question of identity: am I a teacher or a social worker? This question has paralyzed some and frustrated others. Unresolved, it numbs activity and imagination.

Thus far, I've been trying to argue for a tripartite teaching role. Sounds simple enough except for this identity problem. Is the teacher supposed to be a teacher first who gets involved in the community through students and parents (i.e., involvement becomes an extension of the classroom), or should the teacher see himself as a community worker who hangs his hat in the classroom but spends most of his energies and time on the streets?

A sort of schizophrenia splits apart our intern teachers continually. It wasn't enough to caution them that a double vision was necessary—one eye on the classroom, the other on the neighborhood. Such advice was worthless, often resulting in myopia toward one or the other.

It took me some time to figure out what the real issue was. Basically, it is the question: Do the roles of teacher and community worker conflict? Will expecting teachers to work closely with parents and children in the community through home visits and involvement in neighborhood action centers turn them into a new breed of social workers, perhaps subverting their function as teachers? If a teacher organizes a rent strike in a neighborhood tenement, does he compromise his classroom teaching? The answer, I feel, to all three questions is yes.

I see the role of the teacher in the community as analogous to the public health worker whose ticket into the home is health care. The worker has a service to deliver. Most of it is delivered in the clinic or school; some of it is delivered in the home. Both sites must reinforce each other. His chief concern, however, is to improve the health and care of individuals and family. He does not see his job in terms of organizing residents around issues or creating crises or leading the leaderless.

Similarly, the teacher has a service to deliver—the craftsmanship of learning, unperfected but still useful. His clients are students. Most of the delivery occurs in the school but a significant portion must be extended into the homes and community if the service is to be effective. Essential to that effectiveness is the necessity for parents to see the teacher as someone who does, indeed, have some skills to offer and is not just another well-intentioned individual who is bent on "organizing" the community. Of help in this regard would be establishing a study center in someone's home for five kids and helping a parent to eventually run it. Offering concrete skills and advice to help a James and a Deborah improve in school, suggesting what the parent can do and, if the teacher is asked, helping to implement suggestions can be of great use to individuals and community.

With the teacher functioning as a middleman—making rough diagnoses, linking up people with services, training wherever necessary, and building relationships with individuals—confidence in that teacher will grow. As long as the community involvement is seen as an extension of the classroom with the kids as the focus of activities, there should be little danger of a conflict of roles.

On the other hand, if a teacher organizes a rent strike, urges students to boycott a school, or leads a march on city hall he undercuts seriously his role as a classroom teacher. In the classroom where critical thinking and inquiry are supposed to develop and be practiced, advocacy is counterproductive. Parents must have confidence that teachers will not politicize their children for certain ends no matter how socially desirable those ends appear at the moment. The classroom is where questioning, skepticism, and analysis properly belong; advocacy generates a thrust toward dogmatism and indoctrination. Parental and even student confidence will erode when teachers behave as doctrinaire militants rather than as open-minded inquirers.

The distinction I draw between playing the role of social

reformer and effective teacher in and out of the classroom should not be construed as meaning that the teacher mindlessly protects the status quo or sits idly by as events flit past. Teachers should protest when they feel that their rights, as well as students' rights, are abused. Teachers should, if they choose, march and demonstrate. The distinction is between organizing and agitating as a prime responsibility of a teacher or seeing his main job as the intellectual and emotional development of the kids. Responsibility to kids is, I feel, stretched beyond meaning when teachers spend most of their time and energy "organizing" the community and reforming institutions. Yet protest and effective teaching are not mutually exclusive areas. A teacher I know well proved that.

AN EXAMPLE OF A DISTINCTION

He taught in an all-black high school. At the peak of the peace movement in the winter of 1967, his students (labeled "slow learners" by the administration) wanted to know more about the issues in Vietnam. For the most part, as a poll of students and the the neighboring community indicated, President Johnson's policies received wide support; nevertheless, there was a large number of dissatisfied responses.

The class began a study of Vietnam. Other students occasionally stopped in to listen (it was a lunch period), especially when the disagreement grew vigorous. Some of these drop-ins asked for an after-school discussion for those students interested in exploring the topic further. One of these drop-ins, a member of a militant Black Students Union, offered to get a friend who was active in the National Black Anti-Draft Union. The teacher agreed and invited the chairman of the social studies department to present the government position, one in which he wholeheartedly agreed.

With the required information on the activist, the teacher went to the principal since all outside speakers had to be finally cleared by the main office. The principal, upon hearing who the student was who suggested the speaker, reading the biography of the proposed speaker, and seeing the format of the program, refused to let the teacher invite the gentleman on the grounds that he might provoke violence among the students attending. Two weeks earlier, there had been an anti-Vietnam rally outside another school and the police had been called.

The teacher explained patiently that it was to be a debate not a rally, that both points of view were to be presented not a harangue, and that the meeting would be in a classroom holding about 40 people, not the auditorium or stadium. No, again. She was adamant. When the teacher asked if the principal had always had such little faith in students, there was only a scowl and a curt dismissal.

The teacher and the student got together and considered the risks if they held the meeting in the face of the principal's refusal. The teacher was without tenure and the student was a senior; retaliation could be simple and swift. They agreed to pursue it. The teacher arranged another meeting with the principal, wrote out a summary of the first session, and indicated that this meeting was the first step in the union grievance procedure. He informed her that she had deprived him of the right to invite a speaker who, in the teacher's judgment, would help students interested in discussing a crucial issue clarify different points of view. Her reply was still, no.

The grievance was filed. The student was harassed by the principal and her assistant, who began calling in his parents and speaking to teachers about his classroom performance. The social studies chairman was asked to withdraw as a speaker but he refused. Nothing, other than meeting cold stares, happened to the teacher.

The union representative in the school arranged another meeting between the teacher and the administrator. Here, he urged the principal to reconsider her decision, since he felt that the teacher had a good case and the grievance would definitely result in a hearing. After a great deal of talk, she finally agreed to withdraw her objections.

The after-school meeting drew about sixty kids, fifteen teachers, and two parents. It was a crowded and stuffy room. The positions presented by the anti-war speaker and the chairman of the social studies department produced a heated exchange lasting well over two hours. Later, the teacher discovered that the principal had assigned a teacher to take photos of all teachers in attendance and that she had gotten the precinct captain to post two patrolmen outside the doors of the classroom.

What happened to this teacher and the lesson it taught students and other teachers is one of the distinctions I am trying to make between the role of social reformer and effective teacher. The source of the teacher's protest was an intrinsic part of the teaching act; what the teacher stood for was inquiry, not mindless avoidance of controversy. Although the incident was school-based, similar situations arise in the community. Teachers must judge whether their efforts to encourage changes will or will not compromise their effectiveness in the classroom.

Some distinctions can be made, some cannot. There remains a fuzzy area of teaching and community involvement that overlaps and awaits a more precise clarification. Nevertheless, unless the teacher sees himself and his community participation as an extension of what he does in the classroom, the existing gap will widen and inevitably strengthen the teacher's view of the school and community as isolates that bear little relationship to one another.

There is a wide range of activities that falls under the label of community involvement. The visit to the home, however, is the fulcrum upon which any broad-based program of teacher involvement must pivot. Even after the teacher branches out to other activities, it must continue. Indispensable for building personal relationships, the home visit is the basic tool that can narrow the distance between neighborhood and school.

It is a simple device to insure accountability. Anonymity permits callousness and insensitivity to flourish. If a teacher knew the parents of his homeroom students or children in his elementary class sufficiently well so that he could go to their homes or the parents could come to the school freely and without embarrassment, such open communication would go far to eliminate the graceless manners and rhetoric that characterize the controversy over making schools accountable.

This is not the place to list a series of rules on how to make home visits. That an extensive amount of training is necessary for teachers and that parents should be hired to do much of that training seems self-evident. The important point is that the home visit is the tool for humanizing the cold face of the school. There is no replacement for personal and continual contact between parents and teachers.

The current intense feeling over local control and community participation will, if successful in establishing autonomous fiefdoms, still have to confront the same problem of how to get school people interested and concerned about their children. Hiring dedicated people and firing hacks will help some, but ultimately even a locally controlled board representing those who are most vocal will discover that with all their autonomy and power, teachers may not be willing to look outward toward the community; teachers may not feel that it is their job to be concerned about how parents feel about the schools. This is possible, and my guess is that it is probable, since the thrust for local control springs from dissatisfaction with school performance (although grassroots polls have yet to uncover a majority of local residents in favor of community run schools) and a strong push for political control of a very vulnerable institution. The desire to control schools comes from mixed motives and the power to hang the sword of dismissal over a teacher's neck will not extract a competent performance. All of this is to say that there is no guarantee in community run schools or in any school, for that matter, that the professionals will be more responsive to parents and community unless those schools are committed to buy time for teachers to get involved outside the school and provide the teachers with the training required to function in this multi-faceted role. The decisions, as I indicated earlier, could come from a locally controlled board or they could come from the larger school board. There is, obviously, no assurance that it will come from either.

But come, it must. It would be tempting to exaggerate the value of home visits and personal contacts or even to suggest that it is a panacea. But the untapped potential inherent in this tool promises at least to crack the wall of rapidly crystallizing attitudes and positions over schools, race, and community.

BLACK AND WHITE IN SCHOOL AND COMMUNITY

Because home visitation means middle-class whites and blacks moving in and out of the ghetto, it requires extensive training in techniques and intensive probing of one's attitudes. Inevitably the issue of race arises. Because racial attitudes have polarized at a breakneck pace in the past few years, a brief word about white teachers in black schools is in order, especially since I am recommending that teachers of both races make themselves visible in poor neighborhoods.

There seems to be less of a problem with acceptance of black teachers in white schools. Suburban recruitment of Negro teachers has picked up recently. Places like Parma, Ohio, for example, a community that prided itself on not having any Negro residents, recently has hired black teachers. Court decisions have opened up school assignments hitherto closed to black teachers thus, guaranteeing that segregated schools will not have, "accidentally," faculties of one hue. Many fine black teachers heretofore locked into restricted schools have seen more opportunities open up before them. The battle to open up schools and eliminate segregated staffing is still being waged and victory at one point even appeared to be in sight.

Consider what happened in Cleveland. My second teaching job was at a predominantly Negro high school in the Glenville area of Cleveland in 1956. The school had turned from a predominantly Jewish academic school into a middle- and lower-income Negro school within a half decade. By 1956 the process had run its course with students but there was a decided lag as far as teachers were concerned. The first black teacher was assigned to the music department (a coincidence, I was told, not having anything to do with stereotypes) two years before I came. I stayed there seven years and in that time the racial balance on the staff tipped to become largely Negro. Some said that it just happened; black teachers knew better. The rumored policy of the personnel department was to send inexperienced white teachers to inner-city schools and black teachers wherever there were high concentrations of black students. Thus, decades before the slogan—"black teachers for black schools"—Cleveland administrators were believed to be practicing that policy, but of course, for the wrong reasons. Rumors turned into facts after the U.S. Commission on Civil Rights held hearings in Cleveland in 1966. Testimony revealed that Negro teachers comprised only 3 per cent of the faculties in secondary schools that were completely white, while 65 per cent of the teachers in totally black secondary schools were of the same race. When the supervisor in charge of assignments was asked by the counsel to the Commission why this was so, the gentleman responded:

"We find there is a great reticence on the part of Negro teachers to accept this kind of assignment." The court record indicated laughter from the audience. And when the administrator further expained, "They have reacted negatively . . . in saying that it is too far to travel"—the audience must have roared. Everyone there probably knew what the counsel for the Commission then proceeded to point out, that in two adjacent school districts accessible to many Negro teachers, one had mostly black teachers, the other, mostly white teachers. The audience applauded. Rumor had become fact.[7]

Cleveland, Washington, D.C. (as a result of the *Hobson vs. Hansen* 1967 decision), and other cities have undertaken recently a color-conscious policy of assigning teachers, usually following the rule-of-thumb that teachers of one race will not be assigned—provided that qualified candidates are available—to schools where their race is in the majority. An integrated staff has become one benchmark of a quality educational system.

Within the past three years, however, black militancy has produced slogans calling for all-black faculties and control of the schools—all in the name of getting the race together. The purpose is to generate a unity of mind and body so that the race can gain for itself the self-respect and dignity that white America has denied it thus far. The schools will be used to create a racial identity that will, some argue, ultimately produce a vibrant culture. Justification for control is found in the hope of what black people can do unfettered by white presence and, just as important, in the reality of how the white man has brainwashed and bleached the black man of his culture and natural gifts through the public schools. Given this rationale, there seems to be justice in the demand for a proud black mythology to replace the insidious white mythology. Desegregation and integration never worked, the argument runs, because most whites basically didn't want it to work (true enough); let us run our own schools and do what we will with our children.

7. U.S. Commission on Civil Rights, *Hearing,* Cleveland, Ohio, April 1–7, 1966, pp. 364–365.

Obviously, it is from this view that such assumptions as only black teachers can communicate with a black youngster arise. Given these purposes and assumptions, white folk in the school make a cultural revolution kind of difficult. White teachers must go. Thus, polarization which developed out of protests during the 60's becomes a necessary tool to extremists of both races. Black and white have to become monolithic categories, no exceptions allowed, if identity is to be achieved. Is it any wonder that white "liberals" are especially scorned for their subtle racism and that white bigots are praised by black activists for their truth and honesty?

Irony, contradiction, and some nonsense characterize much of this rhetoric about black teachers and black schools. Irony appears in the strategy that activists must use—that is, that white liberal political and financial support is essential for the purposes to be realized. The historical and physical fact remains that the black man is a minority in America, although not in some cities, and that he can go as far as the white majority can be moved. Activists may spit on that fact, rant and rave about it, but that's it. So even the ultimate gesture of disdain for white America—withdrawal, i.e., a separate state—depends upon the white majority's acceding to it. All that remains a fact only as long as the line that is drawn is racial. When the line is redrawn along a socioeconomic axis, it is a new ball game. Allies and coalitions are both possible and essential. Unfortunately, the nation is in the midst of a trend which views every person and event through colored glasses.

Contradiction is seen in the use of analogies. On the one hand, black people are said to be moving through a phase that every ethnic group which has made it in this country has experienced. As the last of a long line of ethnic groups, they have to get themselves together, turn inward, before they can move out and penetrate institutions and begin winning for themselves the respect and tangible success that other hyphenated Americans have obtained. Yet, on the other hand, some point out that Negroes are not like Italians, Irish, and Jews. Black people have been here longer, have been raped of their culture, and are always visible. Abraham Smielgelski can become a Maurice Smith in two generations and no one would have ever known about Ellis Island, greenhorns, and broken English. Not so for a James Jackson. His grandchildren would be considered black regardless of their Harvard degree and suburban home. Both views, obviously, are not mutually exclusive but they do strain against each other.

Nonsense appears in the fantasy that ennobles anything black and decries anything white. Making virtues out of stereotypes—e.g., Negroes are sexier, have more rhythm, are stronger than whites—runs the gamut of exaggeration and error as, for example, one militant lecturing a group of white teachers and principals that only Negro men can really grow full mustaches. Standing near him were two well-mustachioed college professors who happened to be white. What was shocking was that the audience didn't challenge the speaker. He simply continued without pause, while a couple of people snickered at the ridiculous statement. Nonsense appears in the contention that only a black man can teach another black man. Inflating skin color to the single most important variable in teaching destroys credibility. Besides contradicting the science of anthropology—that understanding of other cultures is possible—such a view ignores the ethnic, religious, and racial undertandings and exchanges that have already occurred and continue to occur.

Consider Malcolm X. On his pilgrimage to Mecca in 1964, he discovered that he could break bread with a blond, blue-eyed Moslem and be treated as a brother; the trip convinced him that skin color is less important than point of view. Awareness, not pigment, is crucial.

Black students learn the same thing when they discover, much to their chagrin, that some of the Negro teachers care little for the issues that confront youth today. And it is doubly galling when they see a young white teacher who is not afraid to raise issues of racial conflict, protest movements, and poverty. Bitterly, they wonder who exactly is "white" and who is "black." The mind, not melanin, makes the difference.

The basic question is: What are the aims of education? If it is racial consciousness and proud black people, then the activists are absolutely right; whites cannot teach black people. The teachers can only be racially aware activists who know what they are doing.

Now, are these aims appropriate for public education? I think not. To accept such aims would exclude the openness, the inquiry, and analysis so necessary for teaching and learning. It would require the creation of a curriculum, staff, and style of instruction that would stress the positive, the success story, the victory—a purposely created mythology. And this is propaganda. White mythology in the public schools certainly hasn't worked, and my guess is that replacing it with a black one may satisfy the militants, but propaganda it remains. Acquiring racial awareness and inquiry are mutually exclusive because racial consciousness is an orthodoxy that must be accepted, not questioned. Its place is in the store front, not the classroom. Its teacher must be a true believer not an inquirer, and it can only be taught by a race conscious black man, not a Negro or a white man. And all of this is necessary. Support must be made available. But it belongs to a parochial not a public education. Its place is outside the public schools in after-school sessions like those that CORE and the NAACP have established in various cities, the private schools created by Black Muslims, and in the many store front classes developed by Afro-American societies across the country. It belongs in the community.

That education for racial awareness belongs in the community and should be conducted by black people does not argue for the proposition that only blacks should teach blacks in the public schools. Again the twin strands of political power and dissatisfaction with the performance of the schools have to be recognized. If it is political power that is primary, the slogan of black with black will gain increasing stridency; if it is dissatisfaction that is greatest, then the message is for more effective teachers. Depending on who is making the noises, it is very hard to separate the two strands.

As I said earlier, my hunch is that the parents want good teachers regardless of race. Obvious inequities in recruitment and assignment of teachers must be abolished, but once this has been accomplished the critical element remains the quality of teachers. Furthermore, my guess is that once the rhetoric simmers down, parents do want their kids to learn from teachers of both races. In other words, effective white teachers will disappear from the inner-city only when political decisions supersede the sentiment of most parents and take precedence over the matter of effectiveness. But even then it is doubtful, because as employment opportunities open up for Negroes, fewer will enter teaching.

In 1968, when the Ocean Hill–Brownsville dispute embroiled the New York schools in a series of strikes over the principle of local control, teachers had to be hired to replace those barred by the community school board. The majority of those hired were young and experienced, but white. Presumably, they were hired because of what they could deliver. Effective white teachers do have a definite function in the classroom and inner-city community. There are many middle-class white and Negro teachers who want to teach low-income kids. They should have the same choice that others have as far as employment is concerned. It goes without saying that extensive training must be provided so that the teachers of both races can come to understand the expectations and complexity of performing a tripartite role in both classroom and community.

Being a decision-maker in the classroom, creating and choosing curriculum materials, and being an active participant in the community all require energy, intelligence, and training, a great deal of training. But of the three facets of the teacher's role that I recommend, the time spent in personal contact with parents and members of the community enriches both instruction and curriculum development. Cut off from this function, the classroom becomes pedestrian and irrelevant; the community loses the human touch that schools can ill afford to scrap. Involvement with people can be the hemoglobin that delivers life-giving oxygen to the classroom and community.

Chapter VII

The Inner-city School and the University

In the Introduction, I stated my assumptions about the role and function of the classroom teacher. Two of these assumptions deserve repeating since they are my point of departure in sketching the relationship between the university and inner-city schools.

First: Teachers, regardless of race, who combine intelligence, flexibility, creativity, and concern with a broad knowledge of their students, are involved with them, and are free from arbitrary restraints imposed by the school system, can make a difference with low-income youngsters.

Second: The conventional role of the teacher—i.e., subject specialist teaching five classes a day, or a full day at the elementary level, with extra-curricular activity in addition to all the clerical trivia that burden teaching in an inner-city school—is both anachronistic and self-defeating.

Much of this book is built upon these premises. Conspicuously missing from the analysis, however, is the university's role in producing effective teachers and changing the conventional arrangements in these schools. References to higher education's involvement thus far have had a critical edge to them since I feel that in training teachers for inner-city schools they have failed miserably.

Notwithstanding the significant changes made by some colleges (to be counted on one's fingers and toes) and the small gains made under the aegis of the Teacher Corps, the fact remains that the vast majority of institutions producing teachers have yet to provide them with the kinds of preparation that would do poor children proud. Large state institutions that turn out thousands of graduates yearly scarcely concern themselves with the urgent issues of urban education. A half-hour from the sprawling ghettos of both Washington and Baltimore, the University of Maryland, for example (and a score of other major institutions could be cited as well), recently established a committee (yes, a *committee* a full decade after the poor had been discovered) to study the feasibility of a special program for preparing teachers for urban schools. An urban education effort is planned for 1969–1970. One doesn't know whether to applaud or weep.

Save for a few major universities like Temple in Philadelphia, Hunter in New York, and a handful of others, what ferment there is in teacher education for the inner-city has been generated by the Teacher Corps and smaller institutions located in or near large cities. Programs like the Center for Inner-City Studies at Illinois Teachers College in Chicago; Project Mission, a cooperative effort between the Baltimore public schools and a consortium of area small colleges; and the Inner City Education Project at Central Missouri State College near Kansas City, Missouri, are three such examples. But the ferment has yet to reach the take-off stage. Consider the responses of 281 colleges and universities in 17 southern and border states, including Washington, D.C., when asked whether "teacher training institutions have a special responsibility to help improve the education of the disadvantaged." Over 95 per cent of the universities replied that they do. Fine, except for the response to another question. Asked whether their institution had made any changes in curriculum, faculty, course offerings, or methodology specifically to improve the preparation of new teachers for the disadvantaged, 58 per cent said they had not; 26 per cent did not answer, and the remainder indicated that they had made some changes.[1] The point of all this is what many already know—where the need is greatest, the response by universities has been the weakest.

Some institutions have tried to meet such criticism by creating fifth-year or Masters of Arts in Teaching programs. Other universities, after putting their finger to the wind, have set up a small experimental program under an ambitious assistant professor, and then have sat back and waited until its federal funds expired. The easiest way to check out these efforts is to look for contradictions between the style and content of these programs compared to their conventional

1. *Southern Education Report,* April, 1967, p. 13.

undergraduate offerings. Take Howard University in Washington, D.C., for example, which participates at the graduate level in innovative programs for preparation of inner-city teachers yet continues to offer undergraduate students traditional courses in methods and content divorced from any meaningful involvement in the public schools scarcely three blocks away. Certainly, Howard does not stand alone in this inconsistency. Her sister institutions in the nation's capital are in worse shape. Many institutions speak with forked tongue. Innovative programs to prepare teachers for the inner-city are announced proudly while undergraduate divisions blithely turn out people unprepared for jobs in low-income schools that many will take (and leave). If urban school systems are tough to reform, universities are no bargain either.

The federal government, unfortunately, hasn't gone far enough in unlocking universities from their middle-class, suburban bias. The National Defense Education Act's Title XI (now under the Education Professions Development Act) poured millions of dollars into higher education, subsidizing MAT programs, undergraduate tuition for prospective teachers, and summer institutes for tens of thousands of experienced teachers. To put it crudely, the federal government has given money to many of the very institutions, and in some cases to the same faculties, that have failed to prepare teachers adequately. I see nothing wrong with colleges getting a second crack at trying to improve themselves, but after evaluating over the past four years proposals submitted to the Office of Education for funds, I see precious little progress (as had the survey taken by *Southern Education Report*) in teacher education away from their traditional position toward a firm commitment to preparing teachers for schools where the need is greatest.[2]

There is no doubt in my mind that universities must change fundamentally their teacher education programs because the problem is much deeper than cranking out more teachers for urban schools. Numbers are of less importance than the quality of the training. The question, as always, is change toward what? I have suggested throughout this book the dimensions of a teacher training model. A few words about it are in order.

A MODEL FOR TEACHER EDUCATION

Basically, I see a teacher-education model that is firmly rooted in day-to-day, face-to-face experiences in the inner-city school and community enriched by university support and producing the kinds of knowledge and skills that will be effective in the classroom. Let me hasten to add that the general model I have in mind has many variations: the main thrust, however, involves shifting the center of gravity from the university to the classroom and community.

The model contains four basic components with a myriad of possibilities about how they could be phased in and out. First, content on child growth, the learning process, urban sociology, ethnic history and race relations, and languages of the city must be assimilated—an enormous bank of concepts. Second, one discipline—social sciences, natural sciences, language—must be taken up. Third, the process of re-evaluat-

2. One NDEA project, the National Institute for Advanced Study in Teaching of the Disadvantaged and the EPDA Trainers of Teachers of Teachers (TTT) were anemically funded. The former has expired; the latter limps along.

ing personal attitudes and self-awareness must begin. Fourth, classroom and community must be a crucible of training where knowledge, skills, and self-awareness have an opportunity to be applied, modified, and even created. Last, supervision from practitioners, academicians, and community residents who either teach or are active in the area must be competent and always accessible to trainees.

Baldly stated, the model appears on paper no different from what many educators would point to in their programs. How this model differs from the traditional forms can be seen in a comparison between conventional teacher-education programs and the model I have sketched here. The comparison, by the way, was made by a professor of education, former dean of a large midwestern school of education, and longtime sympathetic critic of teacher-training.

This comparison is not setting up a straw man. Ask teachers about their training. Other than salary, there is nothing more than irrelevant professional education courses that are guaranteed to anger inner-city teachers. (Ah, if only teachers could put themselves into their students' shoes.) Educators will point out to angry teachers that changes are afoot in the university. The model, as described here, is being implemented on a growing scale, many would say. Perhaps the forms, but seldom the substance.

The model tries to narrow the gap between word and deed, to mesh the non-verbal messages sent out by teacher education programs with the rhetoric. Consider what some well-intentioned people and programs say and do. When, for example, the importance of children discovering concepts for themselves is stressed repeatedly through lectures, inconsistency appears. When the importance of knowing your

Model Versus Traditional Teacher-Education Programs

MODEL	*TRADITIONAL TEACHER-EDUCATION PROGRAMS*
Control:	
Centered in school system with cooperation of university.	Centered in colleges with cooperation from school system.
Location:	
Primarily in inner-city schools with commuting to universities.	Primarily on campus with students commuting to local schools.
Approach:	
Practical, inductive, and inquiring, with trainees relating theory to teaching as they work with youngsters in classrooms and community.	Academic, deductive, and didactic, with prospective teachers first learning about teaching vicariously through listening to lectures, reading books, and observing how others teach.
Orientation:	
Specifically to inner-city students and schools.	To general pedagogical theory and practice in white, middle-class suburban schools.
Sequence:	
Professional and academic content is related to clinical experience through group and individual study and personal investigation.	Professional content is treated in formal courses of history and philosophy of education, educational psychology, methods of teaching prior to actual clinical experience.
Clinical Experience:	
a. Responsibility:	
Real—trainees can have responsibility for individuals, small groups, and classes.	Artificial—relationship is that of a visiting observer and assisting teacher throughout.
b. Supervision:	
From competent teachers and academicians who also teach and community residents.	From college staff members who may be years out of touch with actual teaching in elementary or secondary schools and who may never have taught inner-city students.
c. Instructional Materials:	
After training, materials prepared by trainees for inner-city students.	Usually selected by supervising teacher from commercial products.
d. Methods of Teaching:	
Trained in inductive and deductive approaches in line with the needs and interests of students.	Modeled after those employed by supervising teacher or prescribed by college supervisor—with patterns often in conflict.[3]

3. Summary of Traditional Teacher-Education Program taken from Lindley Stiles, *et al.*, "Cardozo Project in Urban Teaching: Evaluation and Recommendations," February, 1967, pp. 13–15.

students well so that wise instructional decisions can be made is matched against the professor's office hours of 2:00 to 3:00 on Friday, inconsistency appears. When the importance of getting involved in the community and knowing its dynamics is underscored yet members of the community are not hired to deal with issues, inconsistency appears. And when the highest importance of public school teaching is continually verbalized by a person who does not teach kids, inconsistency appears.

These inconsistencies are forms of non-verbal communication and as in any classroom tell undergraduates and graduates much more about the integrity of the professor and the particular program than pieties or advanced degrees ever can. Action and behavior carry far more weight than words.

The model suggested here does not guarantee that hypocrisy will disappear from teacher education but with emphasis upon experience and performance and its concern for effective classroom instruction, supervision and community involvement make it possible that a wholeness of word and deed can occur. And that is critical to the success of any program.

Another advantage of this model is its elasticity. To have validity for teacher education, a model must have application to all training experiences, from a two-year course in a junior college leading to an Associate of Arts degree for Teacher Assistants through a MAT degree to a vehicle for systematic staff development programs for career teachers. From pre-service to in-service, the model should be both flexible and effective. But like any model it would be only as effective as the people who execute it are committed to an experienced-based approach. Such commitment implies a redefinition of what is course work, what expertise is, and a conscious recognition that insights produced by involvement in the classroom are as valid and have as much integrity as those produced by scholarly investigation.

Since the New Careers Program, Teacher Corps, the Cardozo Project, and other programs are examples of what efforts might be like at each level of higher education, I would rather sketch out briefly how the model might be applied to one of the most neglected areas of university involvement in the public schools: in-service training.

AN APPLICATION OF MODEL TO IN-SERVICE TRAINING

In too many school systems, in-service training simply involves a few faculty meetings devoted to particular issues, a one- or two-day workshop where experts lecture at hundreds of teachers, or taking courses provided by the school system or area universities. Seldom is teacher behavior changed, the aim of in-service training.

Grounded on an experienced-based model, in-service training programs might be established in inner-city areas (if funds are available, then all schools should participate) along the following lines.

A series of Staff Development Centers (SDC) located in elementary and secondary schools or areas immediately adjacent to them would be established to train classroom teachers and preprofessionals. The aims of each SDC would be:

1. Familiarize participants with current knowledge, skills, and innovations in the teaching and learning processes and plan for their use in the classroom.

2. Identify effective and ineffective methods and mate-

rials for the classroom and implement those identified as useful.

3. Change teacher attitudes and behavior toward involvement in the community and use of methods and materials identified as effective.

4. Provide concrete help and support to classroom teachers and preprofessionals.

Each SDC would either be run by a school system or a university which would contract with the public schools to jointly operate the center. Staff and services from both institutions would be available at the center. Because a university could operate two or three centers and because there would probably be other area institutions willing to contract with the school system, a rich mixture of approaches and personnel would be added to the venture. The resulting ferment could generate a healthy competition to devise and implement different strategies of in-service training.

Sources for staff in each center would, of course, be university personnel who would also have limited teaching responsibilities in the public schools and experienced teachers in the system. (Assignment to an SDC would mean a promotion with salary increase, but staff of SDC would continue to teach part of the day in nearby schools. This would create a status career position for teachers who want to remain in the classroom.) Supervisors and curriculum specialists previously assigned to central headquarters, as is the case in most cities, would work out of a SDC. The interaction between university staff and practitioners in a real, not an artificial, setting would benefit all. In addition, a clinical psychologist, a social worker, and a community organizer would be assigned to each SDC. Each would work with staff day-to-day and face-to-face to equip them and classroom teachers with the skills to understand themselves and the community.

There are a number of ways in which a SDC might function. A few of the possibilities follow.

1. Release teachers for a week, month, semester, or academic year to the SDC and replace them with interns and substitutes who would be trained to take over in instances like this. While attached to the SDC, for example, twenty elementary teachers could spend a week on language arts techniques and materials. At the end of the week, teachers would be expected to produce their own materials and SDC staff would follow up the twenty in their classrooms to help them implement what they have learned and produced.

2. Staff of SDC would teach, observe, confer, and provide assistance to principals who could call upon a SDC for help, say, with first-year teachers. Thus, staff members would be both accessible and visible to faculties at local schools. The non-verbal message is that teaching does count. Being on the staff of a SDC does not mean moving out of the classroom; you continue to teach.

3. One afternoon a week, students could be dismissed early. Students would not lose class time since they would come to school earlier or stay later other days of the week. Depending upon available space, the SDC could use that time for demonstration classes, curriculum workshops, analysis of video-taped lessons, micro-teaching, sensitivity training, lectures, and so on. If space is a problem, then SDC staff could go into the schools to conduct programs.

4. Training experienced teachers, supervisors, and cur-

riculum specialists in the skills of interpersonal relations and supervision should be offered, because teaching competence does not ensure that anyone will function effectively in an assisting role.

5. SDC could operate during school hours, and in the afternoons, evenings, and summers to train all sorts of aides —e.g., teacher, health, social service, recreation, etc.

Although an SDC is a joint responsibility, there are many options for operating particular centers. For example, a university may decide to set up a board of directors composed of representatives of the school system, university, teachers, students, and parents who would hire a director and set policy for the SDC. Another alternative might be the conventional extension of the university into public schools. Opting for a decentralized staff-development operation makes possible a variety of approaches to both managing and directing a center.

University involvement can take other directions beyond joint operation of in-service centers. What is clear to me is that the usual exploitative, paternalistic relationship between public schools and Academe has to end. No longer can schools be regarded simply as institutions to provide the warm bodies for student-teachers' clinical experiences. Universities will have to invest far more of their resources and faculties into the tough business of teacher education for inner-city schools if they hope to become as involved as some of their rhetoric indicates. And tough the job is.

In the last few years, a number of universities have convinced local school boards that they should convert particular "slum" schools into laboratories. Very ambitious in scope, committed faculty at each of the institutions wished to be more relevant. Their experiences as outsiders, mostly white, coming into communities, mostly black, without laying the foundations with students, teachers, and members of the community has been for the most part disastrous. New York University and Yeshiva University in New York City and Antioch College in Washington, D.C. entered with the best of intentions and little awareness or sensitivity to what had been going on in the schools; within a year or two, they were ready to throw in the towel. One university director of a junior high project said:

> We were going to surround the school but it surrounded us. Now we've given up on trying to change the school and are trying to carve out an island in the midst of chaos for the kids we've been working with.[4]

In getting involved, higher education simply hasn't done its homework. In too many cases they have jumped into black communities with both feet, disregarding the expectations of community, administration, and teachers, persistently maintaining a superior-inferior relationship.

Some institutions have tried to avoid this pitfall by seeing their relationship as a junior partner to the school system, providing resources and talent to the schools, or as a broker between state and federal governments in order that identified sources of leadership in the schools and community can function with the assistance of the university. But such efforts are few. At first glance, a senior-junior partner relationship seems paradoxical—i.e., an outside agency trying to initiate change from within by working with the very people who have been

4. *Washington Post,* February 11, 1968, p. C3.

tagged as incompetent and unimaginative. The trick is to parlay university talent and resources and ride piggyback on the sharp individuals who know the school system from inside and for years have been pushing for reform. As difficult as it is, the parlay can be carried off. In this context, universities can operate a sub-system, Staff Development Centers, two year internships for B.A. graduates without certification, a community school, and other imaginative programs. By training teachers in the schools themselves, by improving instruction where it takes place, and by dealing with live people under stress the university can combine their unique characteristics of inquiry, scholarship, and commitment to serve and put them to the test of developing effective teachers and new roles for inner-city teachers. To date, it has been a shotgun marriage with both partners unwilling to see the advantages of the other. Divorce is always a possibility but forced marriages can be made to work, if both parties work at it.

The future of inner-city schools, whether higher education likes it or not, does not rest upon universities getting involved or sitting on the sidelines. Much is, can, and will be done with or without their involvement. The quality of the schools' efforts, however, can be raised or lowered by their presence or absence.

> *"The great difficulty in education is to get experience out of idea."*
>
> —GEORGE SANTAYANA

Index

Index